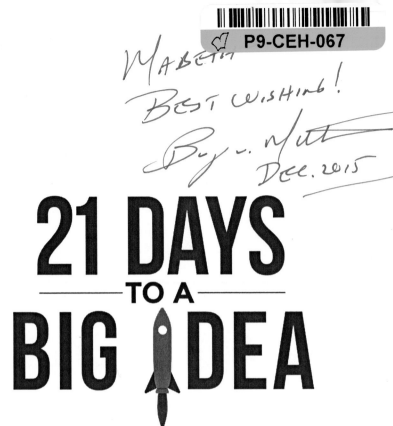

21 DAYS
TO A
BIG IDEA

CREATING BREAKTHROUGH BUSINESS CONCEPTS

BRYAN MATTIMORE

DIVERSIONBOOKS

Diversion Books
A Division of Diversion Publishing Corp.
443 Park Avenue South, Suite 1008
New York, New York 10016
www.DiversionBooks.com

For more information, email info@diversionbooks.com

First Diversion Books edition November 2015.
Print ISBN: 978-1-62681-831-6
eBook ISBN: 978-1-62681-830-9

CONTENTS

For Sri Harold Klemp, Spiritual Leader of Eckankar

ACKNOWLEDGMENTS

I would like to thank:

Bob Dorf, for challenging me to create a "big idea" workshop for his students at Columbia Business School and Launch Gurus in Moscow.

My literary agents: Anne Marie O'Farrell, for suggesting that my "21 Days to a Big Idea" workshop could be a book, and Denise Marcil for insisting that the title be *21 Days to a Big Idea!*

My son James and two of his best friends, Tyler Kane and Michael Whitehead, for pre-testing several of the creative exercises in this book.

Friends Dawn and George Blanchard, and Tara and Chip Archer, for providing thinking and writing retreats at their vacation homes.

My wife Hazel, daughters Caroline and Cathryn, and faithful companion Sami Clyde, for their emotional support throughout the writing process.

And everyone at Diversion Books, for being true partners in the editing, production, and marketing of *21 Days to a Big Idea!*

INTRODUCTION

It was a simple question, more of a challenge, posed during a breakfast with serial entrepreneur Bob Dorf.

If you don't know Bob, he is co-author of *The Start-Up Owner's Manual*, and one of the gurus of the Lean Start-up movement. We both live in Stamford, CT, and it was our volunteer work on the marketing committee for the Stamford Homeless Shelter where we got to know each other well. The shelter's current tag line, "A Haven of Hope," is one result of our collaboration.

Bob had invited me to "get caffeinated" with him that summer morning because he was feeling frustrated. As a professor of entrepreneurship at Columbia Business School and Launch Gurus in Moscow, and consultant to more than a dozen Fortune 500 entrepreneurship teams, he was less than excited about many—if not most—of the "innovations" he was seeing. Whether it was large company concepts or new venture ideas from his students, they were not great. The way he so eloquently put it to me was: "If I see one more idea for a new iPhone cuisine app from my students, I'm gonna burst. There are 850 or more already and this category is growing at a rate of 12–15 new apps a month, very few of which are selling."

He went on to say that he personally interacted with about 750 start-up teams all over the world each year. "If five or eight percent of the ideas in any group are really exciting on day one, that group is at the top of the heap. It's gotta get better on the way in," he said.

Bob knew well my ideation (a.k.a. brainstorming) and innovation work with corporate America, and my book, *Idea Stormers, How to Lead and Inspire Creative Breakthroughs*. He was wondering if "the same powerful ideation techniques in [my] book could be applied to start-ups in large and small companies alike?" This question, in turn, led to his challenge to me:

> "Can you create a workshop that teaches
> people how to generate truly big,
> breakthrough ideas for new businesses?"

I was pretty sure I could. But I was about to leave for a week-long vacation, so I didn't want to commit to creating anything yet. "Let me think about it," is all I said.

My vacation in Cape May, New Jersey, and Ocean City, Maryland, gave me the deep and concentrated thinking time I needed to create a workshop to address Bob's "Big Idea" challenge: a content strategy, specific exercises to deliver on the strategy, and ultimately an agenda.

I know from personally leading over a thousand corporate ideation sessions in my 25-year marketing innovation consulting career, that there are simple yet powerful creative thinking techniques that unleash the creative potential of groups. Whether it is inventing a breakthrough new product or service, creating an innovative new promotion or ad campaign, or even generating creative cost-cutting ideas, these techniques—many of which I will be sharing in this book—have shown time and time again that they inspire "big ideas." And even though the techniques are typically used by groups, I knew that many of them would also work for individuals, since I have successfully used them on myself.

What I didn't know was how to best leverage these techniques so that the workshop participants would be guaranteed to create a big idea worthy of their entrepreneurial effort.

When my company conducts training, we use what's called an "action-learning" approach. It's essentially learning by doing, and we believe strongly in it. So, for instance, at our creative problem solving and ideation technique workshop, we require that each session participant submit a real world business challenge before coming to the training. We match their challenge with one of the dozen or more creative techniques we want to teach. Then in the training itself, participants get to see creative techniques in action, as the group generates ideas—sometimes brilliant ones—to address the different submitted challenges.

Would a similar approach work for teaching 20–25 people how to come up with a big idea in a one- or two-day workshop? Yes and no. A person can learn the creative thinking techniques, yes. But even with an action-learning approach, there was no way to ensure that each entrepreneur would get that one big idea they were looking for. There simply wasn't enough time. It was a question of numbers.

When we lead a new product ideation session, we'll often spend a full day on a single challenge. Typically, we'll generate 150–200 ideas. How many of these are "big ideas?" About 10%. How many of these make it to market successfully after we write initial concepts, qualitatively test them (i.e., in a focus group), and determine their market potential? One or two, if we're lucky. So, it's unrealistic to expect that each of the 20–25 participants in the workshop would leave with "their big idea."

There are other challenges with a one- or two-day workshop. For one, it allows very little time to practice what's been learned. There's also not much of an opportunity for "soak time." This is the time a participant's subconscious needs to make surprising intuitive connections, identify patterns, and make important creative leaps. History tells us that linking two or more previously unassociated elements, leading to a revolutionary new scientific theory or invention, can happen in an instant. Archimedes, Newton, Einstein, Watt, Colt, Whitney, Westinghouse, the de Montgolfier brothers, Carrier, Gutenberg, and countless others have moments-of-inspiration stories associated with their discoveries. But these eureka moments are often the result of intense preparation and focus, sometimes for years.

Given the time limitations of the one- or two-day workshop format, it was clear to me that the workshop would need to teach people a *process* that they could use, over time, to help them create their big idea.

So, I gave myself a creative challenge: to create a 21-day program—one that could be practiced for say, 30–60 minutes a day, much like an exercise program—that would help both individuals and corporate innovation teams learn and practice the creative thinking skills necessary to generate big ideas on an on-going basis. Besides "soak time," I also knew that 21 days would get over the 10% challenge I alluded to: that "only" 10% of the ideas we create in an ideation session are "big ideas." If I could create a three-week thinking program where the goal was "to create at least one big idea each day," then at the end of the 21 days the participant would theoretically have 21 big ideas from which to choose "the best one" for their new, entrepreneurial venture.

Creating a big idea—an idea that is both unique and fulfills an important unmet need–every day for 21 days? Was this even possible? There was only one way to find out. I would "walk my talk" and run the "big-idea" creation program on myself.

One minor detail, though. There was no such program. I would have to invent it as I went along…while also creating at least one big idea per day.

CREATING THE 21-DAY BIG IDEA PROGRAM

As I contemplated the design of the 21-day big idea program, there were three features—call them guiding principles—from my ideation background that I knew would need to be reflected in the program design. They are: "Use Diverse Stimuli," "Leverage a Passion," and "Quantity will lead to Quality."

THE CRITICAL ROLE OF DIVERSE STIMULI

One of the keys to designing and facilitating a successful corporate ideation session is to find—or invent—stimuli that has a high-probability of triggering new ideas. If you're charged with creating a new Oreo cookie, or inventing a new iron for Black and Decker, or a conceiving of a new coffee for Maxwell House—all assignments on which we've worked—it's not easy. These brands have been around a long time, some for over 100 years. So, creating an original concept for a 100-year old brand, especially a well-defined one, requires truly out-of-the-box creative thinking exercises and unique, thought-provoking stimuli.

What kind of stimuli? On a recent new product assignment for a large dairy to invent new milk-based beverages, for instance, the ideation stimuli we used included:

- Pictures and recipes from a book of smoothies
- Photos, descriptions, and samples of unique packages, ingredients, and beverages from a global database of recent new product introductions
- Food and food ingredient trends reports
- Scans of social media comments
- Bartender's "mixologist" guides
- Online searches of expressions, ads, tag lines, book titles, etc. that contain relevant and specific key words such as "refreshing," "nutritious," "healthy," "milk," and "probiotic" juice bar recipes
- Menus from a variety of ethnically-diverse restaurants
- Copies of menus from famous restaurants from late 1800s and early 1900s America (available online from the New York Public Library's collection)

If we recognize that creating something new is often simply a matter of combining "one thing" with "another thing" to get a "new thing," it's not hard to imagine that with this variety of stimuli it would likely (and indeed did) trigger hundreds of new ideas for new dairy-based beverages. How about somehow combining a cannoli with skim milk to create a delicious weight-loss beverage? Crème brûlée with blood orange for an exotic new kind of dessert beverage? Or glazed almonds (in an almond milk form) with probiotic yogurt for a new drink to aid digestion and regularity?

Having the right stimuli to inspire a big idea is critical. But equally important is being passionate about the idea chosen for further development.

LEVERAGE A PASSION

Conceiving of an original new business concept isn't easy. Launching it, and devoting the hard work and creative resourcefulness to make that idea a success, is exponentially harder. If entrepreneurs or corporate innovation teams are going to commit to making an idea a success, wouldn't it be nice to be excited about it? And wouldn't this excitement make it more likely that they'll succeed—that their passion will help sustain them through the invariably tough times and resistance by the status quo and powers that be that so often accompany creating something new?

QUANTITY WILL LEAD TO QUALITY

Brainstorming—though it is often used as a generic descriptor for all group idea generation sessions—is actually a specific technique invented in the late 1930s by Alex Osborne, cofounder of the advertising agency BBDO and driving force behind the Creative Problem Solving Institute based in Buffalo, NY. The two cardinal rules of brainstorming are:

1. Withhold judgment (important to be sure, but often inaccurately characterized as "there are no bad ideas" … which, of course, isn't true at all. Most of the ideas in a brainstorming session, if not necessarily bad, aren't very good either) and
2. Generate lots of ideas because "quantity will lead to quality." This is critical. Osborne knew from his advertising work that there is a tendency to settle for—and stop creating ideas—when the first good idea pops up. I've certainly seen this in my ideation work. I remember a session we did for Coca-Cola to generate promotional tie-in concepts for their sponsorship of an upcoming Winter Olympics. A "virtual-experience" sports tent, just outside the Olympic venue, that would give attendees and, more importantly, the press a virtual experience for many of the Olympic events, was a good idea that was generated very early in the day-long ideation session. But because many of the session participants loved the idea so much, it made it very difficult to get them to create other ideas. They thought they were done for the day, while I knew we were just getting started.

For corporate innovation teams and aspiring entrepreneurs, I wanted to make sure that they wouldn't ever feel that they were settling for the idea they chose to develop simply because "they couldn't think of a better one." A sufficient quantity of ideas would help get around this.

In the scheme of things, the time spent upfront in the

idea-generation phase is so minor compared to the time needed to develop that idea. It seems a shame to me, and I expect to Bob Dorf as well, that his students and corporate innovations teams didn't have the creative thinking tools to help them do a better job at this.

If we go back to our 10% rule, then having at least a dozen big ideas from which to choose the "biggest idea," seemed like the minimum number of ideas to ensure success.

WHAT I LEARNED FROM MY 21-DAY EXPERIMENT

In addition to validating my intuition and ideation experience that "diverse stimuli," "quantity equaling quality," and "arenas of passion" would be important components of a "big idea" program, my 21-day experiment also helped me discover five big idea thinking strategies, namely:

1. What's the problem?
2. Adapt or Leverage a New Technology
3. Help People Self-Actualize
4. Save People or Institutions Money
5. Save Time or Increase the Speed or Efficiency of Something

As we work through our 21 days together, we'll be looking at each of these strategies in depth, including examples of how I and others have used them to create our own big ideas.

Beyond the big idea thinking strategies, I also identified the nine "best" individual idea-generation techniques (among the twenty I considered) that I believed would have the greatest impact on the generation of breakthrough ideas...and be the most valuable for a program in training idea generation and creative thinking. These techniques are:

1. Questioning Assumptions
2. Directed Wishing
3. Twenty Questions
4. The "And" Technique
5. Word Mashups
6. Idea Hooks/Principle Transfer
7. Patent Prompts
8. Trend Bending
9. The Worst Idea Technique

All nine of these techniques are easy to learn, easy to use, and powerful because...well...they work.

In addition to the thinking strategies and idea generation techniques, I also discovered a key psychological consideration in the process of big idea creation. It's hard work. Coming up with a big idea every day for 21 consecutive days is extremely challenging, especially when you have a full-time job. In my case, the first seven days of my experiment, when I was on vacation, were both highly rewarding and a lot of fun. By spending 45–60 minutes a day, I was excited to be able to create several great ideas each day for new products, services, and business ventures.

But by the time I got home, days 8 through 21, things changed dramatically, especially after day 12. It wasn't nearly as much fun. It started to feel like work.

I'll never forget one night, day 15. I was tired from having worked all day on several challenging innovation agency client assignments, and certainly didn't feel like trying to generate another big idea that night. But I had committed to the experiment, so I didn't feel I had a choice.

It was about ten o'clock when I finally got to work. Like the previous 14 days, I had budgeted an hour of reading and creative thinking to generate the day's big idea. I pulled out the magazines I'd planned to use as stimuli that night to help me trigger the idea, and started reading, or, more accurately, "inspiration scanning."

I'm not sure how long it was before I fell asleep, probably not more than 10 minutes. When I awoke, it was 12:30 AM. I had ink on my face. I had been asleep for over two hours, resting on the notebook in which I had planned to record my ideas. I had missed the deadline for my big idea that day. I went back to bed, but before I did, I committed to creating two big ideas...the next morning and evening—which I did.

I tell this story because it's important to know that taking this 21-day program is a commitment, whether it's by an individual or a corporate innovation team. It's work, and there might well be a temptation to quit, much like Osborne's ad men, after generating a few big ideas. But if you stick with it—through both the exciting moments when you create an original idea worthy of further research and development, and the unnerving times when not much seems to be happening and it would be a stretch to call any ideas you settled for that day big ideas—then I think you will be rewarded in two ways.

One obvious "reward" will be a broad spectrum of exciting new ideas, from which you can choose several worthy of further development time and resources.

But as important, maybe even more so, is learning a toolkit of creative thinking strategies and techniques that can be used for solving a wide variety of both personal and professional challenges. Whether it's as a Chief Marketing Officer or social media researcher, small business owner or full-time mom, school teacher or MBA candidate, ad agency creative director or engineer…the creative thinking tools you will learn in this program will prove invaluable not only for career advancement, but even for contributing to a more exciting and fulfilling life replete with the infinite possibilities that new ideas can bring.

HOW THIS PROGRAM IS ORGANIZED

This 21-day program is divided into four sections:

1. Discovering your passion
2. Five creative thinking strategies for discovering idea opportunities
3. Nine creative techniques for generating big ideas
4. Choosing and developing the best ideas

SECTION #1: DISCOVERING YOUR PASSION: DAYS 1–3

This section lays the foundation—both theoretically and practically—for the 21-day program. It will include exercises to help you or your team:

- Build a success footprint, and identify the essential criteria for the winning idea(s)
- Determine the specific areas of passion/ opportunity for the new venture
- Outline the five basic thinking strategies for

generating exciting new start-up concepts
- Understand the kinds of stimuli that will be important for inspiring breakthrough new ideas

SECTION #2: GENERATING IDEAS:
FIVE CREATIVE THINKING STRATEGIES: DAYS 4–8

In Section 2, theory meets reality in the generation of big ideas. It includes exercises and examples of the five creative thinking strategies that I've found useful in generating original products and business concepts. Think of the five strategies as mental lenses or prisms through which your inventive mind can filter—from a world of stimuli such as magazines, trend reports, and TV news programs—the essential nuggets it needs for creative inspiration.

SECTION #3: GENERATING IDEAS:
SEVEN CREATIVE TECHNIQUES: DAYS 9–17

Section 3 is a creative technique boot camp where you'll learn nine of the most effective ideation techniques from the dozens I use in my innovation consulting work. These are the easy-to-learn techniques I've either adapted or invented for the more than 1,000 client ideation sessions I've personally facilitated in the past 25 years. So, I know they work.

SECTION #4: CHOOSING AND DEVELOPING
THE BEST IDEAS: DAYS 18–21

In Section 4, after having created more than a dozen truly big ideas in Sections 2 and 3, you will learn a simple concept-development technique called Billboarding. This will help you to develop your highest potential ideas into easily communicated, testable propositions. By identifying the most important consumer benefit and/or selling point for each idea, you can more easily decide whether an idea merits further research and development testing, time, and money.

Finally, the essential next steps for commercializing the highest potential concept(s)—including how to inexpensively research, develop, and prototype it—will complete the program.

ABOUT THE EXAMPLES IN THIS BOOK...

I know I learn best when theory is combined with simple, illustrative examples. So, in all cases, whether it's to help explain a particular creative thinking strategy, demonstrate a specific creative technique, or provide tips on how to further develop a concept, I've included easy-to-understand examples from my own big idea 21-day experiment, or real-world client ideation sessions. In a few cases, I've indulged my passion for teaching creative thinking and problem solving, by including ideas for new businesses, products or services, or products that do exactly this.

I've also tried not to abbreviate or short-change any of the examples in this book. For instance, when I describe the technique known as Twenty Questions, I include all twenty actual questions. I'm hoping that by seeing the specific details of each technique in action, it will make it that much easier to understand, appreciate, and ultimately apply.

GOING IT ALONE?

As I originally conceived this program, individuals or corporate innovation teams would spend anywhere from forty-five to sixty minutes every day for 21-days to complete it. I knew it would be challenging but certainly worth the invested time. The reward is great: creating more than a dozen big ideas, as well as learning a process for generating these big ideas on an ongoing basis.

And then I realized this program did not have to be taken in consecutive days. Nor would individuals necessarily have to take the program alone. Not unlike the process I'm using to learn to write fiction, the same process could be applied to creating big ideas.

For the past two years, I have been a member of two different young-adult fiction writing groups. There are five writers in each group. Each group meets every four to six weeks to review and offer constructive criticism of each member's writing. It is immensely helpful, not only to hear how I might improve my own young-adult novel (about the misadventures of a group of young inventors), but to hear suggestions for improving everyone else's novels as well. Before joining these groups, I assumed learning to write better fiction had to be predominantly a solitary pursuit. Now I know it doesn't have to be.

The same could be said of creating a big idea. It's obvious that the members of the corporate innovation team will be helping one another, but what of the individuals taking this program? One option is to take it with family, friends, neighbors, students, or a host of other like-minded individuals. If there are writing clubs and investment clubs, then why not creative thinking, "Big Idea" Clubs?

Like my writing group, the Big Idea Club could meet monthly, or even weekly. If the group members are not in a rush, unlike say, Bob Dorf's entrepreneurial students at Columbia Business School who need to create their concept for a new venture quickly, it's not necessary to compress the process into 21 consecutive days. Indeed, having time between exercises might make them that much more productive and fun, and therefore more likely to be completed.

A Big Idea Club, like the cross-functional teams in our corporate ideation sessions, has the advantage of leveraging diverse backgrounds and creative thinking styles: different perspectives, different ideas. It also has a way of exerting pressure on its members to finish their homework/assignments on time. I've certainly found this to be true in my writing groups.

And with today's technology, your Big Idea group does not even have to live in the same state or country. For one of our healthcare clients, for instance, we pioneered the process of leading idea generation and concept development exercises virtually. Eighteen different offices from around the world generated new product, positioning, promotion, and packaging ideas for the company's worldwide pain reliever. Somewhat to my surprise, after we figured out the technical challenges (by keeping things as simple as possible), this virtual ideation process worked extremely well.

So whether you're taking this program with a corporate innovation team, a student work group, friends or family, or by yourself, I wish you luck and excitement, fun and success.

Before you start, I recommend that you and your co-creators get a "Big Idea" journal to record your ideas. Like great inventive thinkers throughout history, by continually externalizing what's on your mind, either in words or drawings, you'll make a greater number and more varied creative connections. Having the opportunity to read and reintroduce your previous ideas with new thoughts from different moments in time will lead to new insights and even several "Aha!" or "Eureka" moments. To facilitate this process of ongoing discovery, make sure you include in your journal not only your daily assignments and the big ideas that come from them, but also any questions yet to be answered, areas in need of further research, potential new arenas of passion triggered by your intuition, trends or interesting data to be considered, preliminary marketing, promotion, and social media ideas, and names you're considering for your new product or business.

One final suggestion: This might be one of the few books you want to read twice. Consider reading it in its entirety, without necessarily doing any of the daily exercises. Then, when you're ready to commit to the hard work of "big idea" creation, you and your team will know what to expect, and be primed to make new creative connections. You'll be familiar with the approach and what's expected of you, so you can focus less on the process and more on generating big ideas.

Now, let's get going!

SECTION #1:
DISCOVERING YOUR INVENTIVE PASSION

DAY #1:
START ME UP!

There's an exercise, a trick really, I sometimes use to open an ideation (or brainstorming) session. It's called an end-of-session excursion. I begin the day, odd as it might seem, by asking each participant to imagine that it is now the end of the session.

"We had a great day. Terrific! Loved it! Couldn't have been better," I enthuse. "Now, what did YOU personally get out of this session?"

There's a bit of psychology built into this simple, imaginative icebreaker. By having each person say what they personally want from the session, it makes it easier for them to give themselves over to the group process. More important, though, it sets goals, expectations and even a success mentality for the ideation session.

Some people, when imagining the end of the session, say it's the best lunch they ever had. But often, and especially for the sponsor of the session, they imagine and verbalize session success.

"We got a half-dozen new product ideas that I can go test and launch," might be one such comment. Or, "We identified several new cost saving ideas that will save our company millions." Or even, "We finally got a strategy that I think—no, I know—will help us turn this division around." It's very powerful to verbalize success.

So, take a moment and do a short end-of-session excursion, or more accurately, "end-of-book" excursion, and imagine what's come of your taking this program. The more specific the better:

- My Big Idea Club has invented three new kitchen products we'll be selling on QVC next year.
- The ad agency I work for has created three fantastic new tag lines for our financial services client.
- Our healthy-beverage innovation team now has three great ideas to compete with carbonated soft drinks.

The examples in this book illustrate how to create big ideas for new inventions, new products, or new services. But the 21-day process can also be used to generate breakthrough ideas for a host of other creative business challenges, including creating a new ad campaign or promotion, generating new selling concepts, or even strategizing a new business model. Whether you're an aspiring entrepreneur or a seasoned corporate innovation team; on your own or working in a small, medium, or large company, the 21-day process should prove invaluable in helping you create your "next big thing."

THE SUCCESS FOOTPRINT

There's another work-from-the-end-backward technique I ask you to try. I call this one "the success footprint." I use it for particularly difficult, even seemingly impossible creative challenges. I think that after you try it, you'll agree it's a great set-up for this program.

The idea of the success footprint is not to try to generate the actual ideas to solve particularly creative challenges; rather to identify the *characteristics* of that successful idea that make it great. So, if you were trying to invent a new game or toy, you'd write down some of the features, or even benefits, about that imagined newly invented game or toy. For example, I used the success footprint technique some years ago to help me invent a new creativity training game. In my "success footprint" I imagined that the game would:

- Help players create things—and be more creative—than they ever thought they could be
- Be fun to play for both kids and adults
- Teach a creative technique or two
- Include endless creative possibilities

and yet, like most great games,

- Have a winner and a loser

Building this success footprint, a kind of "wish with guardrails," was tremendously helpful as I worked through the process of creating what became "Bright Ideas, The Game of Inventing." In the game, players combine specially-selected words to make new, often crazy inventions. The winning and losing comes when players tried to distinguish the player's made-up inventions from little known but ingenious patented inventions from the U.S Patent and Trademark Office.

By building the success footprint, it accomplished three critically-important things as I worked to invent the game:

1. It gave me a way to judge success. If my game met all the above criteria, I'd succeeded. If not, I'd have to keep working on it. So, it helped me be creatively persistent, when it would have been easy to give up.

2. It established for my intuitional mind a kind of creative antennae to the world. By letting myself know—or at least have a feeling—what I was looking for, it increased the chances that I would make a new, even surprising, creative connection.

3. It gave me a specific, more concrete problem to be solved. As such, it helped me ask focused questions, which ultimately led to my new game invention.

So what would your success footprint be for your idea? Spend some time identifying the features and benefits of one or more of your soon-to-be-conceived "big ideas."

- What area is it in?
- Is it a product or service?
- Does it leverage a new or established technology?
- Can I do it myself, or does it require a large team to pull it off?
- It is a business-to-business or consumer product or service?
- Is it a $1 million, $10 million, $100 million, or $1 billion idea?

Despite having no idea what the idea is yet, using your imagination to answer even these very basic questions will help you paint a mental picture—fuzzy as it at first may be—of your idea. As you work through the creative exercises in this book, and generate dozens of possible ideas, the winning big ideas will become that much more clear.

DAY #2:
COURTING YOUR PASSION

Knowing that the creative mind likes specifics to trigger new ideas, I began my "Big Idea a Day" experiment by identifying arenas in which I'd like to create new ideas. And knowing how important quantity can be for inspiring quality, I decided I would come up with at least 50 possible arenas to explore.

Consider the following list:

> Snow compressor, artificial silk, chalk battery, deaf apparatus, electrical piano, artificial cable, artificial silk, box balancing system, artificial mother of pearl, tracing cloth, butter direct from milk, substitute for hard rubber, artificial ivory, pyromagnetic dynamo, motograph mirror, joy phonograph for dolls, phonographic clock, silver wire wood cutting system, ink for the blind, and

red lead pencils equal to graphite.

Oh no, this wasn't my list. These are twenty of the more than one-hundred entries from a five-page list of "things doing and to be done" that Thomas Edison created and recorded in his inventor's notebook on January 3, 1888. It's clear that Edison also believed in quantity equaling quality, as well as the importance of focusing the creative mind with specific creative challenges.

Here's my list:

1) App/Software, 2) Financial/Investment Service, 3) Retail Concept, 4) Restaurant Idea, 5) Entertainment Idea, 6) Game or Toy, 7) Home or Household Product, 8) High Tech/Patentable Idea, 9) Social Service/Help the World, 10) Franchise Concept, 11) Tool, 12) Art Idea, 13) Sports/Exercise Idea, 14) Delivery/Logistics Idea, 15) Business Based on a New Business Model, 16) Energy Idea, 17) Fundraising Idea, 18) Video Game, 19) Idea for Millennials, 20) Gardening or Ecology Idea, 21) Transportation Idea, 22) Idea for Pets, 23) Market Research Service, 24) Furniture Idea, 25) Time-Saving Concept, 26) Idea for Education, 27) Beverage, 28) Food, 29) Cleaning Idea, 30) Counseling/Coaching Service, 31) Life-Stage Concept, 32) Social Media Idea, 33) Insurance Idea, 34) Service/Business for Kids, 35) Service/Business for Older People, 36) On-Line Retail Concept, 37) Business/Service for Artists, 38) Sales Idea, 39) Consulting Service, 40) Webinar Service, 41) Jewelry/Accessories Idea,

42) Service/Business to/for College Kids, 43) Business to Help Teachers, 44) Business/Service for Commuters/Travelers, 45) Business on Better Presenting/Presentations, 46) International Idea, 47) Information Service, 48) Networking Service, 49) Creativity/Innovation Consulting Service, 50) Summer Fun Service, 51) Seasonal Service, 52) Service That's All About Fun, 53) Service That's All About Adventure, 54) Service That's All About Self-Actualization, 55) Service That Teaches Success, 56) Water Sport

You'll notice several important differences between my list and Edison's. For one, Edison's challenges are much more specific. His "to do's" are based on an in-depth understanding of inventive challenges in specific arenas. They also focus on creating inventions, not concepts, for new services or new business models. My list is more generic, almost a naïve wish-list.

Also, unlike most of Edison's creative challenges, my areas are by no means mutually exclusive. For instance, you could create a new international (#46) information service (#47) app (#1) that is all about adventure (#53) and ultimately self-actualization (#54) for college kids (#42).

The point is that whether it's very specific projects, or even more general wishes, you need to start somewhere. A blank page for a corporate innovation team or an aspiring entrepreneur can be as scary as a one for writers or—it seems—even a famous inventor. A list of concrete areas for entrepreneurial creativity, even for those admittedly broad or relatively undefined as mine, can still get the creative juices flowing. As I said to the students at Columbia Business School and in Moscow to help illustrate this point: "Richard Dyson is the only person I know who can create ideas in a vacuum."

Such a list can also help you or your team identify arenas for which you have a passion, and those for which you don't. Research into start-up successes has shown that neither "intrapreneurial" corporate innovation teams nor external entrepreneurs necessarily need specific industry expertise to succeed with their new venture. Indeed, sometimes, especially when trying to create something truly revolutionary, it often helps to NOT have too much industry expertise. But you will need to be passionate about what you're doing. Without passion, the tendency to give up when the inevitably tough times hit will be too great.

So create your list of arenas for new products, services, or business concepts. Strive to generate at least 30, but if you come up with 50 or more, so much the better.

By the way, you'll most likely find that generating these opportunity areas will come in spurts. You'll quickly think of a dozen or so, and then you won't be able to think of any more. Then somehow, you'll get a new one, which in turn will trigger another half dozen. And just when you think you can't possibly think of one more, something in the world around you will trigger yet another idea, which will lead to two or three new ones. Just know that this is how the process can work, and the opportunity arenas most likely will not come all at once.

Why is it so important to create so many areas of opportunity? I'm betting that when you finish the list, creating a dozen or so really big ideas for a new venture won't seem so daunting. With so many arenas of opportunity to consider, the world of creative possibilities should feel like it's opened up significantly.

DAY #3:
FINDING THE RIGHT STIMULI

So, you've done your success footprint for the characteristics of the ideas you want to create. You've also identified the areas in which these successful ideas will reside. Let's generate a few big ideas.

If there's one trick above all others for inspiring a big idea, it's that the right stimuli is critical. What kind of stimuli? Current periodicals in an area of interest is an example of one. Trends from online sites is another. Research reports, international new product scans, award-winning new technologies, and year-end "best idea" summaries from online, key word searches are all good.

A good example of a year-end best-idea summary was reported by *Time*. Israeli inventor Izhar Gafni figured out a way to manufacture and treat cardboard so that it could be lightweight, inexpensive to form/manufacture, strong, and water-resistant. The first product with this new technology: a cardboard bicycle! The entire frame of the bike was made of cardboard. The wheels, chain, gears and pedal were made of lightweight metal. Cost of the bike to make: approximately $12. It was designed to hold a 400-pound person, resist water, and last over two years with normal use.

As a big idea hunter, the bike was fascinating, but it was the opportunity to imagine and invent new products that could be made from this new cardboard technology that excited me the most. This basic technology could be used to create dozens—if not hundreds—of new products. (We'll learn more about "adapting a technology" on day 6.) I decided to go for a run and generate a minimum of twenty "cardboard" ideas before returning.

It's not that easy writing down ideas running—or more accurately lumbering—with pencil and paper in hand, without getting side-swiped by cars, but I did it.

Here's my list of ideas that could use this lightweight, durable, water-resistant, and inexpensive new technology:

A cardboard beach chair, funnel, garbage can, sand sculpture mold, farmer's market/vendor display stand, flower (with seeds in it), kid's stroller, kid's pull cart, bike helmet, beach shoes or sandals, "paper" airplane, commuter's chair, basket weaving set, ice bucket/carrier, megaphone, wheelbarrow, plant holder/pot, wearable "hand clappers" (to magnify the sound of clapping hands at an event), collapsible "wire" racks, game of "Kick the Bucket" (where kids make a contest out of trying to kick winged-shaped cardboard "tents" into a cardboard bucket), skateboard, and 3D jigsaw puzzle.

What advantages would cardboard have in the manufacture or marketing of these ideas? Would they be less expensive? Lighter weight? Easier to carry? Disposable? Easily printed on with colorful designs?

So, how about an inexpensive/disposable pair of flip-flops, printed with fun designs? Maybe these "Fun-Flops" could even be made available free-of-charge to vacationers because they had ads for local restaurants printed on them. Or, how about if the soles of these "Fun-Flops" were molded or formed into cute characters or animals, so with each step an image would be left in the wet sand? Could you make a business out of manufacturing and selling a programmable imprinting machine to local merchants/beach shop owners that could form/customize the bottom of the sandals with a child's name on it? Might be easy to "track down" lost kids at the beach that way, right?

Of the list of the cardboard ideas above, is there one that you can flesh out further as I just did with the "Fun-Flops"?

For my big idea, I picked something other than the cardboard flip-flops. On day 19, I'll share my choice and how I developed it further using the "Billboarding" concept development technique.

For now though, it's important to know that preliminary ideas are just that. Invariably, they need more work before they are worthy of being called a "big idea." And, the most important question to ask of yourself or your team to push your idea to the next level is: What will make my idea both different from and superior to what's currently on the market?

SECTION #2: GENERATING IDEAS: FIVE CREATIVE THINKING STRATEGIES

"For the detective, the crime is given. The scientist must commit his own crime, as well as carry out the investigation."

—Albert Einstein

DAY #4:
WHAT'S YOUR PROBLEM? THE FIRST OF FIVE CREATIVE THINKING STRATEGIES

The Connecticut Invention Convention is a yearly competition among over 10,000 elementary and middle school students to create new and original inventions. In the spring, local and regional winners travel with their parents and teachers to Storrs where, in UConn's fabled Gampel Pavilion, they compete for awards and scholarships from sponsoring companies. As an invited keynote speaker, I was excited to see the best of the best inventions from kids from around the state.

It was clear to me when I toured the hundreds of inventions on display that the predominant strategy the kids used to generate their inventions was, "Find a problem and solve it." This also seems to be the favored technique of student entrepreneurs and amateur inventors, but even occasionally the start-up billionaire. Wasn't Facebook invented to help solve the dating challenges of geeks?

So, how can you use this most-favored of all creative thinking strategies to generate a big idea? Well, step one, not surprisingly, is to find a problem. As obvious and straightforward as this may seem, "problem finding" can take as much creativity as "problem solving," and sometimes even more so. Indeed, framing the creative challenge correctly may be the most important accomplishment of all. Consider what Einstein said: "If I had an hour to solve a problem, I'd spend 55 minutes thinking about the problem and 5 minutes thinking about solutions."

Not to mention that, for us, identifying one or even two or three problems is not going to do it. Since we know quantity leads quality, our goal for today is to discover twenty different problems.

The good news is that we're only finding problems right now. We're not looking for solutions yet. That will come later.

An easy way to create this list of twenty problems is to continually ask yourself during your busy day: "What's the problem?"…"What's the problem?" … "What's the problem?" Much like chanting a spiritual mantra, repeating this simple question should open up new worlds of insight—and ultimately creative-thinking opportunities.

For the corporate innovation team, it could be "everyday" problems like:

1. Consumers don't notice our products on the shelf.
2. The cost to manufacture in the US is prohibitive.

3. Our new products are severely cannibalizing sales of our established brands.
4. We're not finding new channels of distribution for our products or services.
5. Our competitors' products have superior performance to ours.
6. It is not cost effective to sufficiently customize our "master brands" in other countries around the world.
7. There's nothing revolutionary in our new product pipeline.

For individuals, it could be everyday problems such as:

1. My mouth gets dry at night.
2. The best-tasting desserts aren't good for my health.
3. Even with the roller wheels, I get tired of lugging my luggage around the airport.
4. I don't know if the cooked chicken in the refrigerator is still good.
5. My eyes get tired from staring at the computer screen.
6. I don't know where flu germs are.

And the universal problem...

7. I misplace the remote, my glasses, and keys all the time.

Yes, these are certainly mundane problems, but if you could solve them in a uniquely creative way, you just might have something.

Dry mouth? Both Biotene and TheraBreath oral rinses

are designed to help solve the dry mouth problem by increasing saliva production. They remind me of a problem solved by a Minnesota inventor: he had trouble breathing at night. The Breathe Right nasal strip had sales of over $115 million last year.

Is the cooked chicken still good? Experts say you can tell by the smell. Could an electronic device do it better? As Alexander Graham Bell said over 100 years ago, in an address to the graduating class of the Friends School in Washington, DC, "If you are ambitious to found a new science, measure a smell."

Tired computer eyes? Some vision experts maintain that specially-designed computer glasses—which can slightly enlarge the screen, and increase contrast—can indeed help reduce eye fatigue.

Luggage fatigue? There is now an electronic device, with a remote control clicker, that will activate your wheeled luggage to follow you, like a faithful dog, at the airport.

So your assignment for today is to identify 20 problems. These could be little or "insignificant" problems as well as "big ones." In Alexander Graham Bell's same Friends' School address, he ended his talk by saying: "My idea has been to point out to you how great discoveries and inventions have originated from very little things, and to impress upon your minds the importance of observing closely every little thing you come across and of reasoning upon it. The close observation of little things is the secret of success in business, in art, in science, and in every pursuit in life."

DAY #5:
SOLVING PROBLEMS...
AND FINDING NEW ONES

Duke Ellington once said, "A problem is a chance for you to do your best." You've got your twenty problems. Now do your best and come up with some ideas.

Two things to think about as you work through your list: First, there can be many solutions to a single problem. With the "luggage fatigue" challenge for instance, the remote control, follow-me-like-a-dog-on-an-electronic-device invention is one way to solve it. There are many others, and not just new inventions. A service could address the problem just as well, or even better. How about a service, possibly for Silver- or Gold-level frequent flyers that transports your carry-on luggage to your departure gate, or even stows it directly above your seat? Even better, maybe it transports your bags to where you'll be staying?

The second thing to be aware of is that addressing one problem may help you identify other, more interesting or productive problems/opportunities. I like to think of George Bernard Shaw's cynical comment, "Science never solves a problem without creating ten more," as a positive invitation to continue creative problem solving and discovery. A good example of "one small problem leading to another bigger and better one" is the experience of my friend, entrepreneur Micha Weinblatt. In college, Micha would become frustrated when making his bed because, invariably, he'd mix up the longer "length" with the shorter "width." His simple solution was to create a line of bed sheets printed with the letters "L" on the length of the sheet and "W" on the width. Ultimately, he got a Brooklyn manufacturer to make and market his invention.

Micha's "short sheet" problem got him and his childhood friend, Jonathan Schilit, to thinking about how they might address an even larger opportunity. Could they somehow leverage inventive, creative-problem skills in a much bigger way? Specifically, could they create a business that would solicit from an online community of millennials both their problems and their solutions? This led to their creating an online idea generation service called Betterific that has a panel of over 20,000 people, mostly millennials, who submit ideas to inventive contests sponsored by large corporations like Target and Coca-Cola. My innovation agency has partnered with Betterific both for "problem finding" and "problem solving" on behalf of several of our Fortune 500 clients, and it's a great service.

It was Alexander Graham Bell who said, "When one door closes another door opens; but we so often look so long and regretfully upon the closed door, that we do not see the ones which open for us." Micha is a good example of someone who found not one but several other open doors by walking through his first one. A meeting with GE's Chief Marketing Officer, Beth Comstock, led to yet another opportunity for Betterific. It was Beth's idea to use Betterific for *internal* ideation sessions with the company's employees worldwide. These internal, online corporate ideation sessions have now become a significant part of Betterific's business.

DAY #6:
ADAPT AN EXISTING IDEA OR TECHNOLOGY

During my 21-day Big Idea experiment—and the broad reading I did to help trigger big ideas—I came across dozens of interesting technologies.

A Cambridge-based company called Aerodesigns, for instance, has made it possible to now breathe in vitamins, caffeine, and other supplements in 100 milligram doses. Because breathing something in allows it to enter your system very quickly, there is an advantage to breathing in a vitamin like B-12. It will presumably give you the extra energy you may be looking for from a B-12 "shot" almost immediately. The company has also discovered how to make some foods—including chocolate—inhalable.

So as you read this, especially about the chocolate, are there intuitive bells ringing in your entrepreneurial, opportunity-identifying mind?

Could this technology form the basis for the world's

first "deep breathing" diet? Yogis, physicians, self-help gurus Tony Robbins and Deepak Chopra, and founding father Ben Franklin, renowned for taking naked air baths, all have recognized the power and health benefits of deep breathing. Did you know, for instance, that our bodies are designed to release 70% of their toxins through breathing? Less effective breathing equates to more toxins left in the body, leading to a greater likelihood of getting sick.

Combining the health advantages of a deep breathing program with the inhalation of small amounts of appetite-curbing foods makes the new "Deep Breathing Diet" an exciting entrepreneurial opportunity. Developing and perfecting the inhalable-food technology can be left to Aerodesigns. Like Dr. Robert Atkins, or inventor Nathan Pritikin, the larger entrepreneurial opportunity here might be in creating and popularizing the diet itself.

During my "big idea" experiment, I also came across a technology featured in *Discover* magazine on the work of Professor and entrepreneur Dr. John Rogers from the University of Illinois at Urbana-Champaign. Among other breakthroughs, he and his research teams have built soft and flexible "microfluidic assemblies of sensors, circuits and radios for the skin" that can "harvest and store electrical power" from the motions of different body organs. In a kind of second skin, a wireless circuit board could be "printed directly on the skin to monitor a wide range of biological functions including heart rate, skin temperature, muscle activity and hydration." It's not hard to imagine dozens of new products that could come from this technological breakthrough.

Could this technology, for instance, be used to first

monitor and then stimulate specific muscles in the body to help athletes to improve athletic performance?

One way to "adapt an existing technology" is to find a creative or unexpected application of a known technology to create a new product. Another strategy is to use the technology to create a new kind of service. How can you do this in a systematic and proactive way? It's not hard—you simply list as many capabilities, features, points of difference and/or benefits of the technology you can think of, and then look for ways to apply them to different arenas.

Let's take drones, a technology that has received a great deal of press recently.

Among the capabilities, features, and/or benefits of drones are that they can:

1. Rise above traffic
2. Deliver things
3. Give you a new perspective on the world
4. Fly over land or sea
5. Show you what's ahead
6. Deliver things to remote areas
7. Do work in dangerous places
8. Make it easier to do work
9. Find hard-to-find things
10. Interact with the air
11. Provide feedback/information/data from a unique perspective
12. Communicate with other drones
13. Hover overhead and record things
14. Protect people or animals?
15. Attract attention, make something special/unique

Can you think of five more benefits for drones? How about using our five creative thinking strategies: two of which you've already seen, three which you'll be introduced to on days 7 and 8?

Could drones...

16. Identify and/or solve problems?
17. Adapt or possibly combine with another idea or technology?
18. Save money?
19. Save time/make something more efficient?
20. Help people self-actualize?

Can we then combine these capabilities and features of drones with arenas of passion to create new products or services?

In the health field, "flying over traffic" could certainly save time if someone needed immediate medical attention. Medical drones are now being equipped with first aid kits, including defibrillators. Combining "health" with "flying over land or sea" might trigger another idea currently in development: a kind of "flying lifeguard" drone that can drop a life preserver to a swimmer in trouble.

Combining "hover overhead and record things" with "help people self-actualize" might suggest a new sports training service, used by coaches or as part of marketed video sports training program, that could now use drones to give athletes an overhead, three-dimensional view of their performance.

Could drones also be used to create a new advertising service, such as one that starts small with flying promotions for local advertisers before launching a new national advertising service made possible by a fleet of thousands of "ADRONES?"

Your assignment for today: 1) find one or more new technologies that intrigue you; 2) list at least twenty capabilities, features, points of difference, and/or benefits of this new technology; and then 3) combine it with one of your arenas of passion to create a new product or service concept.

DAY #7:
SAVE MONEY, SAVE TIME

On the seventh day of my 21-day Big Idea experiment, I came across a front page story in the Sunday edition of the *New York Times* by reporter Elisabeth Rosenthal entitled, "For Medical Tourists, Simple Math." The story's subhead: US estimate for a new hip: $78,000. The Belgian Bill: $13,660. The article told the story of Michael Shopenn, a 67 year-old architectural photographer and recreational snowboarder who needed a hip replacement. The pain was so bad that he "couldn't stand long enough to make coffee, let alone work." But medical insurance wouldn't cover the joint replacement because it was related to an old sports injury and was therefore considered a "pre-existing condition." Because of the prohibitive cost of an operation in the US, Mr. Shopenn explored other options overseas, and ultimately chose a private hospital in Belgium for his operation. Here is a further breakdown of the cost differential:

- Hospital Room: US $8,050 (three days). Belgium: $3,700 (five days).
- Implant: US $36,861. Belgium: $4,200.
- Surgeon's Fee: US $17,500. Belgium: $1,110.

His Belgium cost also included all doctor's fees, operating room charges, crutches, pain medicine, a week in rehab, and a round-trip ticket from America.

The difference seems outrageous doesn't it? And if, like me, you were reading this article with an entrepreneurial mindset, it's not much of a creative stretch to imagine there might be a new business opportunity here. How many successful businesses have been made by saving consumers either money or time?

To dimensionalize the possible opportunity, and build it out into a well-developed business concept, the Questioning Assumptions technique (which I'll say a great deal more about on day 10 of our adventure together) can be tremendously helpful. The Questioning Assumptions technique will force a depth and diversity of thinking that can help the aspiring entrepreneur or corporate intrapreneur conceive of both how the service might work, as well as its possible points of difference.

So here are twenty assumptions I made about "medical tourism" as I worked to develop this perceived cost-saving business opportunity into a big idea.

1. Quality medical care is difficult to obtain abroad.
2. The US has the world's best hospitals.
3. Americans get the best medical care from exhaustively trained, highly experienced specialists.
4. The best medical technology is in the US.

5. Most Americans would be resistant to traveling overseas for an operation, even with the potential cost savings.

6. Doctors abroad are less well-trained, experienced, or skillful as US doctors.

7. Communicating—and the lack of locally available support from US relatives and friends—could be a problem.

8. US Hospitals will not help patients coordinate with foreign hospitals for these less-expensive procedures.

9. US health insurance plans will not cover operations overseas.

10. There might be a limited market for overseas operations since medical insurance now covers most operations, anyway.

11. There is no real incentive for patients who have insurance to travel overseas for an operation.

12. It would take a great deal of work to find and vet the best overseas hospitals.

13. Government regulations—both in the US and abroad—would make it extremely challenging to create a viable overseas medical operation service.

14. It could be difficult to coordinate a rehab program in the US if the operation were performed overseas.

15. US and foreign doctors might not "speak the same language," figuratively and literally.

16. This new service could garner a great deal of free publicity because of the dramatic

cost difference.

17. There would be tremendous resistance—and even an effort to discredit this new service—from the US healthcare system.

18. Fluctuating exchange rates would make it difficult to know exactly how much an operation overseas would cost.

19. Since this would be a new service, it might be difficult to find the data needed to "prove" that having an operation overseas is a safe alternative.

20. Having some operations (knee or hip) might be easier to promote in an overseas location than others (heart or kidney transplant).

Which of these assumptions are "true?" And which are "false?" I'm not sure. But by simply listing these assumptions, it helps raise essential questions about how this new service could be structured, and ultimately what its point of difference could be.

Furthermore, asking whether the assumption is true or not misses the point. Just because something is "true" today, doesn't mean that it can't or shouldn't be changed in the future. Even more important than being true or false is that the process of identifying these assumptions will provide direction for further concept-development thinking and market research.

Let's look at four of these assumptions in light of their concept-development potential.

Assumptions 10 and 11: "There might be a limited market for overseas operations since medical insurance now covers most operations, anyway"; and "There is no real incentive for patients who have insurance to travel overseas for an operation" naturally bring to mind the idea that healthcare insurance companies could create a program to incentivize patients to have their operation overseas. Maybe they share the savings? If Michael Shopenn hadn't had a "pre-existing condition," and his insurance company was contractually-obligated to cover his operation, the company would save almost $65,000 by encouraging Michael to have his operation overseas. So, counterintuitive as it might seem, the insurance company would then be wise to *pay* Mr. Shopenn—say...$10,000 or $20,000—to have his operation overseas because of the $40,000 or $50,000 they'd save by him *not* having his operation in the US.

Consider assumption number 12: "It would take a great deal of work to find and vet the best overseas hospitals." If this is true, it could be the basis for an important competitive advantage, a barrier to entry by potential competitors, and an effective PR and communications campaign. Our new service, having invested significant time and money to identify, enroll, and possibly sign exclusive contracts with the world's best hospitals and doctors outside of the US, could achieve a significant first-mover advantage over potential competitors. And the results of this research might surprise even the most geocentric American researchers. After all, America has no claim on having the best healthcare in the world. Indeed, in a recent survey by the Commonwealth Fund of ten other countries and the quality of their overall healthcare, the US ranked *last!* (1. United Kingdom, 2. Switzerland, 3. Sweden, 4. Australia, 5. Germany & Netherlands (tied), 7. New Zealand & Norway (tied), 9. France, 10. Canada, 11. United States).

Finally, consider assumption number 8: "US Hospitals will not help patients coordinate with foreign hospitals for these less-expensive procedures." What if we questioned this assumption and considered the possibility that a US hospital, or chain of hospitals, could indeed partner with foreign hospitals and act as a referral agency—for a fee—for these less-expensive overseas medical procedures. It could be a relatively low-cost, high-margin new profit center for these US hospitals.

Could you use a similar Questioning Assumptions approach to generate a new business concept around saving time? What are some time or efficiency challenges you have? I'm assuming managing too many emails is on your list. Like me, did you assume little if anything could be done about it?

Mike Song questioned this assumption and founded a company called GetControl.net, designed to help busy executives get control of their emails. By using a variety of ingenious tricks, tips, and shortcuts—including little-known email features that let you filter, categorize, and segregate low-priority emails from high-priority ones—his training has been shown to save managers, on average, 30 minutes a day—or 15 days a year!

There are two steps in your assignment for today. First, identify a half-dozen money and/or time wasters either from your personal life, your work, or something you see in the world, hear on TV, or read in the newspaper/online. I think you'll find that once you make a conscious decision to look at the world with a time- or money-wasting (or saving) "mental filter," you'll discover challenges/opportunities everywhere. For instance, this morning I read in my local newspaper that our mayor was concerned that the city was spending too much money in overtime for city workers.

Step two is to then pick one or more of the money or time wasters you've identified and see if you can create a new business or service to address the challenge. For instance, thinking about overtime, could you create a software program that would enable managers to more efficiently align available employee time with city work that needed to be done, and therefore, potentially help cities around the country save hundreds of thousands of dollars a year?

DAY #8:
FACILITATE SELF-ACTUALIZATION

I'm a baby boomer. I don't feel old, but facilitating a new product ideation session for Chobani yogurt recently, with most of the marketers in the room half my age, means that I, along with the 76.4 million other baby boomers born between 1946 and 1964 in the US, might indeed, be getting old. What unique needs do baby boomers have?

How about the 80 million millennials in the US, those born between years 1977 and 2000?

Or the Gen X-ers, those born between 1965 and 1980? (Clearly, experts don't all agree on the exact age delineations for these groups.)

If I think about myself and the rest of the baby boomers, it is clear that health and mental acuity will become increasingly important as we age. What new products or services can help me and my baby boomer buddies?

Great ideas can often be found at the intersection of new

technology, cutting edge research, and an emerging trend, or in this case, demographic shift. What new product or service could you or your corporate innovation team invent to help baby boomers self-actualize—or at least remember where they put their keys?

The online brain-training site, Lumosity (along with others such as Jungle Memory and CogniFit), is a wonderful example of a business fulfilling this need. Lumosity cofounder Michael Scanlon, while a PhD candidate in neuroscience at Stanford, had the bright idea to bring to the public "brain games," derived from cutting edge research in neuroplasticity, which is the brain's ability to reorganize itself by forming new neural connections. His passion to understand—and help people improve the functioning of their own brains—was driven in part because both his grandmothers suffered from Alzheimer's. Today, Lumosity has over fifty different scientifically researched games designed to improve memory, attention, speed and mental flexibility, and over 50 million members.

The question you might ask then: "Is there research that can be taken out of the laboratory—and used as the foundation for starting a new business?"

Psychologist Dr. Leo Flanagan has leveraged cutting-edge scientific research to help him create his new business, The Center for Resilience. When the terrorist attacks happened on 9/11, Dr. Flanagan put his corporate consulting and coaching work on hold to counsel survivors and rescue workers who were suffering from post-traumatic stress disorder (PTSD). He did the same thing for families of the Sandy Hook shooting and victims of Superstorm Sandy. In the process, Leo came to understand that the burn-out factor and PTSD symptoms he was seeing in many of these victims, he was also noticing in his corporate clients. He resolved to do something about it.

The mission of The Center for Resilience, a program built on scientific evidence from MIT, Stanford, and Harvard, is to help busy, often overworked and stressed-out executives achieve both greater job satisfaction and peak performance. Research shows that professionals in demanding careers operate at only 32% efficiency. So in an 8-hour day, only about 2.5 hours is highly-efficient work time. Using tools and techniques from the cutting-edge research, Dr. Flanagan's program equips these executives with the life tools they need to reduce stress, be happier, and, in the process, double their efficiency and effectiveness at work.

Beyond cutting-edge scientific research, how else might you create a product or service to help people—old or young—to self-actualize?

Have you heard of the Genius Box? It's a subscription service that, for $25 a month, sends kids age 8–11 a box of cool stuff so they can conduct experiments and do activities around a particular STEM (Science, Technology, Engineering, and Math) subject. Crystals, kaleidoscopes, gravity, and magnets are four of the topics/boxes that have been explored so far. Wummelbox has a similar monthly subscription model providing creative arts and crafts projects for kids 3–8.

Then there's BKFK Education (By Kids For Kids). Founded by my friend Norm Goldstein, this Stamford-based company creates and manages educational and creativity contests for kids. Three sponsored contests to date have encouraged kids to: invent school supplies for Staples, create new backyard games and exercise equipment for Sports Authority, and start a new business in the "Grow Your Own Business" Challenge from Warren Buffet's financial literacy initiative, sponsored by Experian.

With information, knowledge, and even insight and wisdom now so freely available online, can you think of any way to curate, organize, and/or package this information to create a new service to help people self-actualize? TrendHunter.com, which you'll hear more about on Day 15, in addition its trend reports, has a free offering that groups hundreds of online speeches into themes or categories. So, for instance, TrendHunter.com provides links to 100 videotaped talks on entrepreneurship, 20 on designing innovative products, 26 on creating start-ups, 20 on business models, and 100 on branding. There are additional talks grouped by such categories as health and fitness (56), technology (83), and charity (30). If health and fitness is an area of interest for you, it's hard to imagine that after watching these 56 videotaped speeches, you or your innovation team wouldn't be able to think of a half-dozen concepts for new products or services in this field.

In my innovation consulting work, we're now using short excerpts from speeches by subject matter experts as a way to inform and inspire creative thinking in our strategic planning and creative idea generation sessions. It used to be that companies would hire these experts to a give a motivational speech at $10,000 or more a day. Now, a free five-minute video might suffice. For instance, in an ideation session we designed and facilitated with a large bank's top one-hundred executives to "reinvent how we go to market," we used short clips from interviews with business mavericks like Lou Gerstner or Steve Jobs to set up several of the creative exercises.

Is there a business opportunity here? Could you create a service that categorizes and assembles clips from the tens of thousands of online speeches, MOOCs, subject-matter experts, and YouTube videos to meet the content needs of meeting planners? A slightly different version of this idea that came out of my 21-day Big Idea experiment was to create a company that would promote, on behalf of large advertisers, "crowd-sourced" video creation contests. Not unlike BKFK Education or even Frito-Lay's contest to create Super Bowl ads, this company would manage all aspects of the video-creation contests, including contests to benefit causes with which the organization might like to be associated.

Your assignment for today is to watch a variety of online speeches, presentations, or even YouTube videos from subject matter experts in one of your areas of passion. Then, based on what you're seeing, hearing, and learning, create at least one big idea for a new product or service that will help people, teams, or organizations "self-actualize." And don't forget, once you have your idea, you can use the Questioning Assumptions technique to help you further dimensionalize it.

SECTION #3:
GENERATING IDEAS:
SEVEN CREATIVE TECHNIQUES

DAY #9:
WISHING FOR THE IMPOSSIBLE...
AND THEN MAKING IT REAL

There's a famous, ten-year research study in the world of creativity. Futurist and author George Land had five year-old kids take the NASA creativity test. He then had them retake the test off and on over a ten-year period. The results were both startling, and depressing. When the kids were five years old, 98% of them tested at the highest level for creativity. At age ten, the percentage of kids who were still testing as creative genius had dropped to 30%. At age 15, the figure was 12%. What could account for such a precipitous drop in creativity? It was clear to the researchers that school, and the emphasis on getting the single "right answer," was to blame.

As educator Neil Postman said, children enter schools as question marks, and leave as periods.

In the creativity consulting work we do, we often

encourage our clients to try to rediscover the fantastical thinking they were so good at when they were young. It's not easy. As adults, we've been trained to be hard-nosed realists. We've come to see the wishful thinking we did as kids as impractical or stupid, and generally a complete waste of our valuable time.

The irony is that when adults can recapture the unbounded and unlimited imaginings of their childhood, important breakthroughs, even billion-dollar industries, can be the result.

So, Mr. Bell, you want to talk through a wire. Good luck with that. A spacecraft that will travel fifty times as fast as a speeding bullet? Yeah, right. Have access to every book ever written or song ever sung in a device that will fit in your pocket? Dream on, fellow.

Author and futurist Arthur C. Clarke said, "Any sufficiently advanced technology is indistinguishable from magic." So your assignment for today is to create 20 wishes, the more magical the better.

The key to succeeding with this exercise is to push beyond the mundane or practical…and wish for the impossible. An easy trick for helping do this is to fantasize about things that could violate a law of nature.

As I worked through my 21-day program, here were some wishes I had:

I wish…

- I could inhabit the body and mind of twenty-one different famous people for the next three weeks.
- I could take an imaginary/virtual-reality tour of Moscow before getting there.

- I knew the people/friends that strangers and I have in common.
- I could experience a day in the life of one of my parents when they were 18.
- Companies would post their creative challenges, just like they post their job vacancies.
- I could brainstorm new ideas with help from great people in history.
- Fruit tasted as good as ice cream.
- The YouTube videos, which were essential viewing for my career, were packaged and sent to me daily.
- I knew what my body needed for me to eat at any moment in time to make it as healthy as it can be.
- Scientists would call me asking for help with their toughest challenges.

If you or your corporate innovation team is looking to find an idea you could turn be a billion- dollar business, the wish technique could be the technique you're looking for.

Start by generating your twenty wishes. The more "out there" and seemingly impossible the better.

What comes after you've generated these wishes? You invite back the hard-nosed, reality-based part of yourself that was so well-trained in school to help you turn your fantasies into realities. There are a couple of questions we've found useful for helping you do this.

First, you might ask yourself, "As absurd or impractical this wish is, is there some way I can make it a viable idea?"

The second, more pragmatic question to ask: "Is there something I can take out of or be inspired by in my wish that will lead to a new idea?' With the first question, you're trying to make the impossible idea real. With this second question, you're using the impossible idea to help you think of a different idea.

So, work through your wishes to create several big ideas. Let me give you an example of how this might work. Let's say you've decided that one of your areas of opportunity/ arenas of interest is in home repair. What then are some wishes you could start with?

I wish I could...

- let people see how hundreds of different colors of paint would actually look on their new house.
- paint the house with light.
- paint the house with a paint that would change color in different weather...or with different moods of the owner.
- change the color of the house with a remote control/clicker.
- paint someone's house with a paint so durable that it would never have to be painted again.
- "paint" the house with pre-fab, stick-on decals that would make it a work of art.
- paint the house with different themes for the holidays.
- paint it with invisible paint so burglars didn't even know the house was there.
- make it easy for young kids to paint the house.
- peel off the old paint (yes, it's peeling) to reveal a brand new coat of paint underneath.
- use a flying jet pack, instead of a ladder or

scaffold, to paint the upper floors of the house.

- put an attachment on my garden hose that would let me paint my entire house just by "watering" it.

Next, we want to take some of these wishes and turn them into real ideas—or at least avenues for further research and discovery. Some ideas naturally follow from a wish. Others take more work.

Could you create a line of stick-on decals (removable or permanent "House Prints" or "Home Art") that would let you to customize the look of your house? Sure, why not. Maybe large decals for the holidays or to create a "magical castle" of your home for the young kids in the family. How about a trompe l'oeil (or trick of the eye) door to confuse unwanted callers?

Have you seen the NeverWet spray-on coating by Rust-Oleum, or the "Always Dry Wood and Stone" product by Nanex. You can use them to paint invisible messages on a sidewalk or paved driveway. The messages appear, like magic, only when it rains!

A bit of magic that might take more work: Create a paint that never has to be repainted. A seemingly impossible wish, but maybe it could inspire you to invent a new, long-lasting paint. Could a study of the more durable paint used on bridges or other hard to reach or hazardous environments offer a clue? Maybe nature could provide an answer? Understanding and transferring the processes nature uses to solve its design challenges (a field now known as bio-mimetics, literally mimicking nature) might help you look at your long-lasting paint challenge in an entirely new way. Consider that peacocks don't hire feather painters. And yet, their plumage is always bright and beautiful.

So, instead of thinking about a paint that never has to be repainted, maybe a better question is: "How, like nature, can I invent a paint that will repaint itself?"

Peacocks "repaint" themselves by regrowing the colorful feathers that have fallen off. So, could you invent a "living paint": one that uses microorganisms, acting like skin cells, to replace the outer layer of "peeling" dead skin? Admittedly, a crazy idea, but is it any crazier than any of our modern-day miracles?

Maybe you could somehow transfer the recent research findings and technology that have enabled scientists to create clothes that are literally alive. Known as biofabrics, an article in *Popular Science* reports that researchers are working on garments that have a layer of living cells that "feed off dead ones" so the fabric can clean and repair itself. Imagine, then, if you're cold, the cells in your garment "might reorganize just as feathers and fur fluff up at act as insulators." Couldn't we do the same thing for house paint?

Your assignment for today: Push yourself to imagine twenty impossible wishes in one of your areas of interest. Then, take several of these impossible wishes and turn them into two to three potential new business concepts. Don't worry about how developed or even practical these ideas are yet. Further thinking, research, and development will come later.

DAY #10:
THREE IDEAS IN THIRTY MINUTES: THE QUESTIONING ASSUMPTIONS TECHNIQUE

We got our first glimpse of the Questioning Assumptions technique on Day 7 when we used it to develop what I'm calling I-MONE, the International Medical Options Network concept. Besides being great for developing ideas, the Questioning Assumptions technique is also wonderful for inspiring the initial big idea.

As its name implies, the Questioning Assumptions technique is about uncovering possibilities for new ideas by questioning the assumptions we make about anything and everything in the world around us. So for example, what are the assumptions we make about a chair? Well, let's see.

A chair...

- has a back and four legs
- should be comfortable

- "sits" on the floor

And the most basic assumption of all:

- is for sitting in.

Turns out every one of these assumptions has been questioned...with the resulting new product features or inventions to match.

A chair with a back and four legs? Can you have a chair with three legs? Yes. Two legs. One leg? Yes. Yes. No legs and no back. Think of bean bag chairs. When would you want a chair to be uncomfortable? How about at McDonald's where you want to keep folks from lingering and the tables turning. Could you have a chair that doesn't sit on the floor? What about the swing chair attached to the ceiling by a chain or rope?

A chair that isn't for sitting in? Ever heard of a standing chair? The Standing Task Chair website says it does a great job of supporting your body "while it's in a standing position."

There are two particularly interesting things about the Questioning Assumptions technique and the ideas it can inspire. For one, sometimes the most obvious assumption can be difficult to identify. In retrospect, the assumption that a chair is for sitting in may not have been the first assumption you thought of. That's why when you do this technique it's important to generate a minimum of fifteen to twenty assumptions for each challenge.

The second thing is that by making the assumption conscious and explicit, generating ideas that follow from the questioned assumption can be quite easy. As an example, let's take a picture frame.

We assume a picture frame...

- holds a picture
- hangs on a wall or sits on your desk
- is made of material different from the picture
- holds something essentially flat, like a painting
- "frames" the picture
- frames one picture at a time
- has its presentation side on the same side as the framed picture
- should either aesthetically add to, or certainly not detract from, the picture it frames
- needs a way to secure it to a wall or stand on a desk
- helps preserve the painting, document or picture by covering it, often with glass
- is made of solid material
- has one design
- is used for a single purpose: framing a picture
- has a top, a bottom, and two sides
- should be larger than the picture it is framing

And even, in some ways, the most basic assumption of all is...

- that its reason for being is to actually frame something, but not necessarily only a picture.

So, having questioned these assumptions, what new ideas come to mind? Could we manufacture and market a new line of picture frames that...are entirely electronic? Can be programmed to have changing designs? Consist of projected light and/or lasers? Hang not on walls, but in mid-air (possibly with repelling magnets)? Is curved or even spherical? Or that has secret compartments to hide valuables?

Before getting to the today's idea assignment, let me give you a real world example of the power of Questioning Assumptions in yet another common, even mundane, category: toothpaste. This one is courtesy of my Growth Engine co-founder, Gary Fraser.

Before Gary and I cofounded our innovation agency, Gary led the oral care division at Unilever. He had three brands: Aim, Pepsodent, and Close-Up. Together they had about a 12% market share of the billion-dollar oral care business in the United States. Compare this with market leaders Crest and Colgate, together accounting for over 60% share of the market. How could Gary compete with these hundred-pound gorillas?

The metaphor Gary used to describe his competitive challenge was: "Crest and Colgate owned the field, the ref, and the fans. The only way we could hope to compete and ultimately win was to change the rules of the game."

So how do you change the rules of the game, especially in an established, even pedestrian, category such as toothpaste? One way is that you question assumptions.

What are some of the assumptions about toothpaste in general, and more specifically how it's made, packaged, and marketed? Here are a few.

Toothpaste...

- cleans and whitens teeth
- prevents cavities
- comes in a tube
- sells for about $2.00 to $3.00 a tube
- has GRAS (generally recognized as safe) ingredients

As all good marketers do, Gary and his team had looked in many places for new product ideas: trends, new technologies, products from foreign countries, patent searches, innovations in other categories, etc. In the toothpaste category specifically, they considered entirely new ways to clean teeth (i.e., ultrasonic technology) as well as different kinds of nontoxic cleaning ingredients (vinegar, baking soda, lemon juice, etc.).

But it was only when they combined this searching with a willingness to question their assumptions that they discovered their breakthrough idea.

Gary's team knew about a "kitchen remedy" in the toothpaste category. In the late 1800s and early 1900s America, an inexpensive way to clean teeth was to mix a small amount of baking soda and hydrogen peroxide in your hand. It tasted awful, but it worked great. The release of oxygen when the peroxide reacted with the baking soda did a wonderful job of both cleaning teeth and keeping gums healthy.

Could the team create a new, better-tasting hydrogen peroxide and baking soda toothpaste that would also release the gum-healthy oxygen? It took literally years of work by the R & D team, but eventually the chemists thought they had solved the problem. They encapsulated the peroxide in the baking soda base. The idea was that the friction from the brushing would shatter the encapsulated peroxide and then, and only then, create a chemical reaction to release the oxygen.

To make sure the formulation was stable they did what's known as a ship test. Tubes of the new toothpaste were boxed and shipped in trailer trucks to different parts of the country. The 120-degree heat inside the truck in the middle of a Georgia heat wave caused the toothpaste's ingredients to react prematurely, and blow out the back of the toothpaste tubes. When the driver opened the back of the truck, there was toothpaste everywhere.

It would have been easy at that point to give up, but they didn't. The breakthrough came when they questioned the assumption that toothpaste had to come in a tube. If you've ever seen or used Mentadent toothpaste, you know it comes in a stand-up dual dispenser. The baking soda and peroxide ingredients come out in two separate streams and meet for the first time on the user's toothbrush. Before Mentadent was sold to Church and Dwight in 2003, it achieved annual sales of over $150 million and Gary was named Marketer of the Year by Brandweek.

Your challenge for today: Pick something from your arena of interest, either a product or a service, and generate twenty assumptions about it. Then create three ideas for a new product or service inspired by these questioned assumptions.

DAY #11:
20 QUESTIONS, ONE BIG IDEA

One of the fifty magazines I bought during my summer vacation "big idea" experiment was *AARP*. It's been more years than I'd care to remember since they began sending me mailings to join their organization, so my resentment toward their invitations has mellowed with age. In addition to a cover story on Gloria Estefan, and her "thirty years of hits," other articles in the magazine included: "The Health Care Act, 10 Big Changes," "Take Charge of Your Money at 50+," "Surprise, Workers Get Better with Age," and "Bill Clinton, His Life-Saving Diet."

Reading these titles with an entrepreneurial eye, any one of them could be fodder for "big idea" creation thinking. Might Clinton's healthy weight-loss program, for instance, give other famously named diets such as Jenny Craig, Perricone, or Atkins a run for their (significant) money? What if 10% of the profits from the new Clinton Diet company profits were donated to organizations to help fight child obesity?

"Surprise, Workers Get Better with Age," was the article that most caught my creative interest and attention. The subhead to the piece is: "You should hire this guy. Why? Older workers have strengths that can make them the most valuable people in the office. Here's the surprising truth about experienced employees."

So, older workers have a problem getting jobs? And companies would be pleasantly surprised by their strengths? Sure sounds like an opportunity for a new kind of executive recruiting, or a temp service: one that specializes in placing workers over 60 years old. Shall we call it the Grey Wolf agency? Probably preferable to naming it Silver Fox, which might be mistaken for an over-60 escort service.

How can you move beyond the first "obvious" idea to create one with greater uniqueness and added benefits to a potential customer? A technique we use in our corporate ideation sessions to both address difficult creative challenges and to push preliminary ideas into becoming developed concepts is called Twenty Questions. Like the other techniques in this book, it's easy to learn and use, but also powerful in its results.

Twenty Questions is similar to the Questioning Assumptions technique in that you generate a list of questions to help you think about your creative challenge differently. Instead of creating a list of assumptions for your challenge, however, you simply free-flow a list of questions, that could either suggest other possibilities or dimensionalize the current challenge in new and different ways. An easy way to create this list of twenty questions is to begin each question with what I call a possibility prompt: "How can _____", "What are _____", "Could we _____", "Is there _____", "How about _____", and even "If _____."

Here are the twenty questions I used to help myself think more deeply, and consider more options, for the Grey Wolf temp agency concept.

1. What are older people uniquely qualified to do?
2. How can a company get to know an employee without hiring them?
3. How can a prospective employee get to know a firm?
4. How can an employee demonstrate their value—without the employer making a big commitment?
5. How can we increase the prospective employee's value?
6. If the prospective employee could work as a temp, how could they provide immediate value to the organization?
7. Could you reinvent temporary workers: not just office skills, but efficiency consultants?
8. Could the temp service administer a whole battery of tests, not just typing, to identify unique abilities of a temp?
9. What could we call the temp agency service that specialized in finding work for older people?
10. Could this be a more competitive, higher-priced temp agency?
11. Could the older employees be used to question the assumptions of what everyone is doing in

the organization they are assigned to?

12. Could older employees become mentors to younger employees?
13. Could these mentors be quickly and easily trained to learn new, valuable skills?
14. Is there some combination of mentoring and providing immediate value/worth to the organization?
15. If they were a mentor, how could they make the process more efficient for the time-starved worker?
16. Could the mentors be trained in time-saving tips to teach others to be more efficient with their time?
17. Could the older employees read things for their bosses to help them get caught up?
18. Could "time-savers" shadow an executive for a week to help make them be more productive/ have more fun?
19. Could a time-saving consultant be focused on certain specific areas: managing email, making meetings more efficient, prioritizing, etc.?
20. Could an older employee be trained in and then coach: Interpersonal/Leadership Skills? Idea Generating Techniques?

You'll notice a theme emerging from this eclectic, free-flow of questions: How can older, temporary office workers expand their role and organizational contributions beyond simply typing and filing?

The increased time demands on middle and senior

managers, coupled with waning corporate loyalty has meant a decline in the mentoring of younger workers. Could older, experienced temporary workers close this "mentoring gap" by helping new employees to think more strategically, and communicate more effectively?

Could specially trained temps, beyond fulfilling the daily requirements of typing and filing, also help individuals and departments be more productive? This became my "big idea" for the day: A temporary agency called Time Bandits that offers older temporary workers specially trained in time management, organizing, and other productivity processes and tools. It's a nice combination of the self-actualization and saving time creative thinking strategies.

Your creative challenge for today is simple. Take something of interest you or your corporate innovation team has discovered from a recent reading of a magazine or newspaper and subject it to the Twenty Questions technique. You may well discover that in the process of asking—and then answering—your twenty questions that: a) you will create a surprising and exciting new idea or, if you already had an idea in mind, that idea will be b) significantly improved!

DAY #12:
EXPECTING THE CONNECTING:
THE "AND" TECHNIQUE

If you had only thirty seconds to create a new invention, could you do it? What if I upped the ante a bit, and asked you to create this new-to-the-world invention—again in thirty seconds—in front of 200 people? How about then?

This was exactly the situation in which I put fifteen brave volunteers not too long ago. And you know what? Each one of them did it! Was this an audience of professional inventors? Corporate innovators? Engineers? Scientists? Creative artists? No, it was a group of librarians!

This all started when I got a call from Joan Levey, special projects coordinator for the Chicago Public Library System. Once a year in Chicago, they close down the entire library system for a day of learning and enrichment for their employees. The theme that year: creativity and innovation.

Joan was curious if I might like to be a keynote speaker at their event. I happily agreed, even though I would have to deliver my keynote three times, since the hall in which I'd be speaking could only accommodate 200 at a time.

I kicked off each of my three keynotes with my inventors' challenge with five volunteers. How did they all successfully create a new invention in only thirty seconds? If you think back to Day Three of this excellent big idea adventure, you'll have the answer: it's "stimuli." I gave each volunteer two inventor's cards from my Bright Ideas training game. All the cards had different word triggers on them, but they were similar in that on the first card were six concrete nouns: i.e., "lamp," "pencil," "bed," "phone," "sock, "and "finger;" and on the second card were three other concrete nouns: i.e., "wristwatch," "window," and "bathtub;" and three adjectives: i.e., "elastic," "illuminated," and "reversible."

The librarians created their inventions by simply combining a word from card one and a word from card two. What's an "illuminated sock?" It's one with glow in the dark paint so you can either find a matching pair in the early morning when you're getting dressed…or you look cool when walking at night. A "bathtub pencil?" A specially designed waterproof marker that you can write ideas down on the bathtub or the shower wall. Or maybe it's a pencil with a secret compartment you can fill with "bathtub gin" and drink surreptitiously at less-than-exciting management meetings? A reversible wristwatch? It's a wristwatch with a band that you can flip to a different color to match your mood or what you're wearing that day, much like a reversible belt.

The purpose of this simple exercise was not to generate a great invention—although in some cases that has actually happened. Rather, it is to demonstrate that with the right kind of mental prompting we can all be creative. Since creativity is so often a self-fulfilling prophecy—if we define ourselves as creative, we're more likely to continue working on a creative challenge until we get an answer—it's very important that we do indeed see ourselves as creative.

Want to try it? You've got ten minutes to invent ten new inventions.

Here are four inventor cards to help you. Use the first two cards to get your first five inventions. And the second two cards to get your second five inventions. Go!

Inventor card # 1: "t-shirt," "music," "jar," "pants," "sand," "ring"

Inventor card # 2: "sidewalk," "globe," "wallet," "lighted," "cooling," "illustrated"

Invention #1: _____

Invention #2: _____

Invention #3: _____

Invention #4: _____

Invention #5: _____

Inventor card # 3: "string, "sunglasses," "puzzle," "flashlight," "ball," "pillow"

Inventor card # 4: "comb," "paper," "marbles," "liquid," "magic," "heated"

Invention #6: _____

Invention #7: _____

Invention #8: _____

Invention #9: _____

Invention #10: _____

How'd you do? If you pushed yourself to create really good—even great—inventions it may have been tough. But if you let yourself go, and allowed yourself to play, and even be a bit silly, you were probably able to do it, and even have fun in the process.

Can you use this combination exercise, the "And" technique as I call it, to generate your big idea? Probably not. It's a little too random and unfocused. But it's great training in creative connection making, since most ideas—even big ones—are simply a matter of combining one thing with another thing to create a new thing.

The way you *can* use the "And" technique for big idea generation is to focus it. To do this, simply make half of the "and" be an area in which you or your corporate innovation team have an interest—or better yet, a driving passion.

Here are two real-world examples of how I've used the "And" technique in my innovation consulting work:

In a speech I gave to Asocolflores, the association of flower growers, in Bogotá, Columbia, I suggested they link "flower" with "opportunity categories" as I called them—twenty in all—to create a host of new products, marketing, and promotion ideas. So combining "flowers" with categories such as: "sports," "food," "education," "hobbies," "travel," "historical events," "luxury goods," "celebrities," "emotions," "greeting cards," "religion," "fund raisers," "contracts," and "new distribution channels" made it easy to generate a wide range of ideas they hadn't considered. "Flowers and celebrities," for instance, brings to mind the obvious idea of a signature bouquet—endorsed by a celebrity—much like the Open Hearts pendant designed by Jane Seymour and marketed by Kay Jewelers. "Greeting cards and flowers" might suggest a joint venture with a greeting card company to include specially themed and designed cards with each flower arrangement? Or maybe include gift certificates for flowers at a local florist with a greeting card. You get the idea.

Another example of how I've used the "And" technique is a new product development assignment we did for Chips Ahoy! cookies.

So, Chips Ahoy! cookies *and* other great treats? Chips Ahoy! and…ice cream? Chips Ahoy! and…candy? Chips Ahoy! and…cakes? Chips Ahoy! and…even other cookies?

Have you seen some of the varieties of Chips Ahoy! cookies on the market?

Reese's pieces Chips Ahoy! Mint Chocolate Chip Chips Ahoy! Birthday Frosting Chips Ahoy! Chips Ahoy! with Oreo filling. Many of these "and" ideas were on the market before we starting working with them. But one of the "ands" that we helped them create was Brownie Chips Ahoy! It proved to be one of the highest-scoring concepts in the brand's history, and has become a high-margin success for them.

The important point is that thinking of your area of passion with an "and" (versus say, an "either/or") can pay huge dividends.

So your assignment today is create five new products or business ideas by combining a word that represents an arena of great passion for you, with words that you find by opening to random pages in a dictionary.

DAY #13:
SMART MOVE: BENEFIT WORD MASHING

There's a word combination technique we use in our corporate ideation sessions called semantic intuition. It's an interesting technique because it triggers new ideas by having participants "name an idea first—and then figure out what that newly named idea might be." Crazy, right? Naming an idea before you know what that idea is? It seems counter-intuitive, especially for a technique named semantic intuition?

You might be surprised that as strange as the technique sounds, there is a precedent for it in the creative arts. Songwriters (for example, Sting) will at times create a song title first, and then use the title to inspire the song's content. Neil Simon named his play "The Odd Couple," before he wrote it. *Chicken Soup for the Soul* authors Jack Canfield and Mark Victor Hansen will test dozens of book titles before they commit to actually writing the book. And "B" movie producers in the 50s would often create a title and poster for a movie, and test the poster before committing the money to actually make the film. One wonders if today's horror and comedy "classics:" Gingerdead Man 2: Passion of the Crust (2008), Surf Nazis Must Die (1987), and S.I.C.K. Serial Insane Clown Killer (2003) might have benefited from such pre-testing.

With the semantic intuition technique you will randomly combine words from three different categories to trigger a new idea. So for instance, if you were trying to invent a new dairy-based concoction, you might combine kinds of dairy products (yogurt, soy, almond milk, cottage cheese, sour cream, etc.), with interesting ingredients/flavors (chocolate, walnuts, blueberries, acai, calcium, coffee, toffee, etc.) with different kinds of packages, food or beverage forms/carriers (tub, straw, bottle, tea bag, can, plastic tube, gum, etc.). These randomly combined word triads (one word from each column) are then used to inspire your new product ideas. So, for example, if you were doing this exercise in 1998 and your word triad were "yogurt", "blueberry," and "plastic tube," it might well have made you think of a new, on-the-go yogurt for kids. You might even have called it Go-Gurt, along with the tag line: "the first ever portable, low-fat yogurt in a tube" that makes "on-the-go snacking slurpably fun."

Today, "almond milk," "coffee," and "gum" might inspire you to think of a healthier, less expensive, and more convenient alternative to a hot- or iced-coffee afternoon pick-me-up. How about a delicious, super-premium, highly caffeinated cappuccino, espresso or latte gum that sells for four times the cost of a normal stick of gum, but one-tenth the cost of your $4.00 Starbucks Grande Vanilla Caffè Latte?

An even simpler version of semantic intuition, one we

call "Word Benefit Mashing," is to combine a single, specially selected word modifier with your area of interest or arena of passion. Because "Word Benefit Mashing" combines two sets to words to inspire new ideas, it is similar to the "And" technique. However, because the modifiers are specially selected to be benefit-oriented, the technique tends to be both efficient and effective. In this case, we will be looking for benefit modifiers that reflect one or more of our five creative thinking strategies: 1) Find a problem, 2) Facilitate personal growth or self-actualization, 3) Save people or organizations time or 4) Money, and 5) Adapt an existing idea or technology to a new use.

Here are ten such modifiers:

1) smart/thinking, 2) speed/quick, 3) educational, 4) informational, 5) healthy, 6) virtual, 7) digital, 8) futuristic, 9) mobile, 10) growing/expanding

Of these ten, "smart" is one of the most productive and "on-trend" for generating "big ideas." Since I don't know your team's area of passion, let's word mash "smart" with ten common household objects: "Smart cup," "Smart lock," "Smart pen," Smart shirt," "Smart beer," "Smart basketball," "Smart spoon," "Smart helmet," "Smart mixer," "Smart bicycle."

Does modifying these everyday objects with the word "smart" give you any ideas? If I told you that at least three of these word mashups were actual products/technologies, either currently on the market or planned for launch shortly, could you guess which ones they were?

Before continuing, see if you can invent a new product or two or three inspired by these simple word mashes.

How'd you do? Which of these smart inventions are actual products? Turns out all ten of them are.

What's a smart lock? There are now a variety of electronic bicycle locks that you can open with your smart phone. And you can share the app/code with others who might want to borrow your bike, so they don't need a key either.

A smart spoon? When I hear "smart spoon," I think of a spoon that has a sensor and microchip in it so it can tell you the calorie count of food you are about to eat. The Liftware Spoon is actually a "smart utensil" specifically designed for people with Parkinson's disease. Created by Lift Labs (now owned by Google), the spoon's embedded technology can automatically monitor how a hand is moving, and make adjustments to help keep it balanced. Shaking is reduced by an average of 76%.

How about a smart basketball? There are now several on the market. Like the smart lock, sensors tie into an app on your smart phone. The 94/Fifty smart basketball, for instance, can help a coach train his players to take faster shots. The audible call-out immediately lets them know how quickly it takes the player, once he catches a pass, to shoot. A second after catching a pass is too long. Seven-tenths of second or less is good.

And finally, what about a "smart beer?" Smart water, yes…Glaceau's pure vapor distilled water with added electrolytes. But a smart beer? Not sure the how well "smart" links with "beer." Well, a European firm says it does.

The beer is called The Problem Solver, and the Danish brewing company's website claims that "beer-loving researchers have proven that when reaching an alcohol level of precisely 0.075% the average person produces the most creative thinking." That's why the company says it has "brewed a beer especially made to bring you as close to your creative peak as possible. All you have to do is drink and think." In a bit of creative package design, possibly derived from taking their own beer-drinking-in-moderation advice, the company has printed an indicator on the bottle that "makes it easy to find your creative peak" by drinking "the amount that fits your weight to make sure you hit the magical 0.075%." They also caution that your creative peak could quickly turn into a creative valley if you drink too much.

Of course, mashing the modifier "smart" with your team's arena of passion is only one of the ten modifiers listed above. You could also use modifiers that take you to a whole new level of fantasy—and opportunity. "Smart" bicycle helmets, for instance, will sound an alarm if a rider hits the ground. If the alarm is not deactivated it will automatically alert emergency contacts with the rider's location. But what about thinking of say, an "invisible" bicycle helmet?

A Swedish company has created an invisible bicycle helmet by incorporating an air bag into a comfortable neck collar that automatically inflates if it senses the rider is falling.

We all know invisible dog fences. But what about invisible braces? Invisible headphones? An invisible car?

Your creative challenge for today is to invent one "big idea" in an area of passion by mashing it up with one of the benefit modifiers: 1) smart/thinking, 2) speed/quick, 3) educational, 4) informational, 5) healthy, 6) virtual, 7) digital, 8) futuristic, 9) mobile, or 10) growing/expanding. And remember that to create a big idea you may have to generate five or more smaller ones.

DAY #14:
TRANSFORMATION TRANSFER:
IDEA HOOKING AND PATENT PROMPTING

Let's say you and your innovation team have identified a problem you'd like to solve. And you've even generated several solutions. But none of your ideas either work particularly well or are significantly better than what is currently on the market. How do you discover that elusive point of difference, or "better way?"

If you're like many of the greatest inventors in history, you try to identify and transfer the principle from something from another area to solve the challenge in yours. Looking for ways to manufacture your cars faster and cheaper? If you're Henry Ford, a trip to a slaughterhouse gives you your answer. You adapt the principle of moving carcasses on chains around the "disassembly plant," as it was known in those days, to moving your car chassis, also on chains, to more quickly and efficiently assemble your cars.

Let's look at three related, but different "principle-transfer" creative thinking strategies from three of history's greatest inventors, and then see how you and your innovation team can apply them to your development challenge.

The year: 1793. Connecticut inventor Eli Whitney is visiting Catharine Littlefield Greene, widow of the Revolutionary war hero Nathanael Greene, on her Georgia plantation. The problem that Whitney felt needed solving: how to remove seeds from cotton.

So he keeps the challenge at the forefront of his mind, and everywhere he goes he looks for principles or mechanisms of action that could solve his problem of how to remove seeds from cotton.

Mrs. Greene is making Eli eggs for breakfast. She scrapes the frying pan with a spatula. Could he somehow scrape the seeds off the cotton with a spatula-type device? Not sure.

The workers on the planation are boiling wood ash lye and animal fat to make soap. Could he dissolve the seeds by boiling the cotton and adding an acid of some kind? Probably not. Forget it. Bad idea.

And then it happens. Whitney sees a cat reaching through a fence trying to grab a chicken, and even though the cat only came away with a few feathers, he has his eureka moment. The idea is to create an "engine" (or "gin" for short) that uses prongs on a wheel to "grab the cotton"—much like the cat's claw, and then use a bar, much like the fence, to knock the seeds off the spread out cotton. And this is indeed how Eli Whitney got the idea for the cotton gin.

So, like Whitney, one way to solve your problem is

to keep it top of your mind, and continually search for analogies that could trigger a solution. In our work, we call these idea hooks. These are concrete objects or experiences your brain can "hook onto" consciously or occasionally even subconsciously; identify the inherent principles or mechanisms of action of a thing, and then apply those identified principles to solving your challenge.

You can look for these analogies as you go about your day…or you can increase the odds of finding a solution by reading broadly, with a principle-finding/principle-transferring state of mind. Case-in-point is the 19th century inventor and industrialist George Westinghouse. Train travel in Westinghouse's day was dangerous because even though engineers might see an approaching train, often their brakes were not good enough to prevent a collision. Just such a head-on collision actually happened to Westinghouse on a trip from Schenectady to Troy, NY. So, he set to work trying to invent a better braking system. But none of his initial ideas proved practical. They were either too clumsy or generated too much heat.

And then he happened to read a magazine article about a tunnel being bored in Switzerland. The Swiss engineers were using a rock drill connected to a compressor that was over 3,000 feet away from the actual drilling—deep inside the mountain. Westinghouse immediately made the connection between the principle of "remote power delivery" from the rock drill and a better braking system he could deliver along the entire length of the train. The air brake was born and wound up saving countless lives.

So looking for analogies or ideas hooks in your everyday experience is one solution finding strategy. Another is reading broadly. A third idea is to look to nature for solutions...the field that today has come to be known as bio-mimetics.

Before there was even a term for it, there was the brilliant English inventor and engineer, Sir Marc Isambard Brunel (1769–1849), who would often look to nature for inventive inspiration. In addition to inventing machines for sawing and bending timber, making boots, and knitting socks, he also invented the "tunneling shield" enabling him to dig the first underwater tunnel under the Thames River at London. He got the idea by watching how a shipworm tunneled through a wood timber. The shipworm's up-front shell plates allowed it to both bore through the wood and push the sawdust out behind it. Brunel built a similar giant shield by using screw jacks that could be pushed through the soft ground under the river.

A more recent example of looking to nature for inventive inspiration is the Stickybot, a wall-climbing robot that, by imitating the flap-like ridges on the toes of a gecko, has "feet" with directional adhesion that enable it to easily climb a smooth surface like a glass wall.

Whether it's looking to nature like Brunel, reading broadly like Westinghouse, or simply keeping the creative challenge top-of-mind like Whitney, the creative mind has the ability to transfer the principles or mechanisms-of-action inherent in one thing to potentially solve challenges with another thing. It's as if the mind is at once a kind of radio transmitting and receiving station. We send out creative challenges to the universe, and if our receiving antennas are attuned to the right station, solutions are sent back.

One question we might ask then is, "Do we have to wait for inspiration to strike?"

The answer is no.

Without having the luxury of waiting for eureka moments to occur by chance on client assignments, I wanted to invent a creative technique that we could use proactively to discover solutions to different product engineering challenges. The technique I created, Patent Prompts, takes advantage of a relatively recent offering by the United States Patent and Trademark Office (USPTO); namely that their database of patents can now be searched by key words. All patents issued by USPTO from 1976 until the present are available, free of charge, online.

So, let's say you've just read about the flap-like ridges on the toes of the gecko, and decide it might be fun to try and invent a toy that could walk up walls. Searching the key words "toy" and "wall" reveal that there are 9,341 US patents since 1976 that have these two words in them. US Patent # 8,979,609 B2 for instance, is a "Wall Racer Toy Vehicle." This invention uses battery-powered fans to create a difference in air pressure around the chassis of the vehicle which "urges it against the surface" allowing it to operate on both walls and ceilings.

US Patent # 8,639,400 B1, is "Altitude Control of an Indoor Flying Toy," bounces signals off a wall to maintain a "selected level for the vehicle." Could this invention be used to make it appear that a toy is "walking" on the ceiling? "Suction Wall Climbing Toy with Articulated Body Segments," US Patent # 8,371,898 B1, with a "drive wheel that rotates" and flexible-mounted appendages that "allow for the illusion of climbing." And then there is US Patent # 8,328,368, B2, "Projection System," which enables a table or wall lamp to project images on the wall or ceiling and act as "a pet entertainment device." Could you make something appear to walk on the ceiling with a projection?

So, the patent prompt technique can help you solve your creative design challenge by considering a wide variety of different ideas and technologies.

Your assignment for today is to:

1. Identify a challenge associated with the design or engineering of one of the new inventions you've conceived in taking this program.
2. See if you can crystalize this challenge into two words.
3. Search the USPTO patent database using these two key words.
4. Scroll through many of the often thousands of patents that your key word search will most likely generate, looking for inspiration to solve your particular challenge.

So, if you have an idea for a _____?_____, and it requires a quick-release connector to make it a viable new invention, you might search the USPTO patent database using the words, "quick" and "connector," and discover that there are over 42,000 patents issued from 1976 to the present that contained these two words. That should give you something to think about, right?

The hope is that by reviewing the relevant patents, you will discover a new "connect and quick-release" idea, that you can somehow adapt—without infringing the existing patent—to solve your particular design challenge.

DAY #15:
GETTING HOTTER ALL THE TIME:
TREND BENDING

You and your innovation team know the arenas in which you'd like to create a new product or service. You've internalized the five creative thinking strategies: find and solve a problem, adapt a technology, save time or money, and help people (or organizations) self-actualize. You've questioned assumptions, wished for the impossible, and mashed together a variety of provocative word modifiers within your area of entrepreneurial passion, and yet you still do not have as many big ideas as you might like to choose from for your entrepreneurial (or intrapreneurial venture.) What now?

The simple answer is to get more and different stimuli to trigger your inherent connection-making ability. You'll want to continue to read magazines and online articles in a wide variety of fields to find, and possibly transfer research, insights, and/or ideas to your areas of interest.

A related but different "more stimuli strategy" is to use the trend research available on the internet. The companies that specialize in trend reports charge fees for customized studies, but will often make other trend information available free of charge. Cassandra Daily has a free, online trend alert. Mintel, the global new product reporting service publishes a free consumer trend report each year. JWT, the global advertising agency, makes available online annually a free trend report "100 Things to Watch in [fill in the current year]." And TrendHunter.com has a newsletter and monthly trend report that lists thirty to fifty new products and/or trends in different categories such as fashion, technology, design, business, ecology, culture, life, and even "bizarre" … also for free.

TrendHunter.com is especially interesting because they will crystalize an identified trend into two-word essences, a process similar to both the "And" technique and "Benefit Word Mashing." Here are examples (from a video on TrendHunter.com) of seven "two-word" megatrends: "Responsive Retail," "Ritualized Collaboration," "Biometric Capture," "Swap Commerce," "Waste Currency," "Practical Printing," and "Routine Rental." See if you can guess what they might be.

Let's take a look at a seven trends included in the JWT report in the past few years to see how we might "bend the trend" to a specific area of interest or opportunity.

The trends I picked fall into the creative thinking strategy of helping people self-actualize. They lend themselves to creating both new services and new products:

1. Intellectual, artistic gaming: "a new wave of intellectual, artistic, and poetic video games"
2. Experiential artistic spaces: "multisensory experiences that augment nature and public spaces"
3. Thought leadership tourism: getaways to learn about "technology, science, the human spirit, and civilization"
4. Sensory literacy as core curriculum: programs to teach people "how to speak visually"
5. Mindfulness in classrooms: teaching students to "be completely present in the moment"
6. Contemplative computing: using information technology and social media to help us be "more mindful, focused, and creative"
7. Sports mashups: combing two sports for a "unique recreational experience." Think of playing a game with a soccer ball on a golf course.

How might you or your innovation team push your thinking on, and around, these trends to create unique and ownable new products and services? Some of the creative techniques we've already covered could certainly help: Twenty Questions, Directed Wishing, Benefit Word Mashing, and Patent Prompts, to name four. But there's another creative thinking technique that could work as well, or sometimes even better when "bending trends." Think of this technique as a kind of disciplined Twenty Questions. It's the "5 W's and H" technique. By asking who, what, when, where, why, and how, of these and other trends, the chances are very good you will discover an exciting, and unexpected new business opportunity.

Let's see how exploring questions from the "5 W's and H" technique can unlock new creative possibilities.

Take the trend of "mindfulness in the classroom." Two firms, Inner Explorer and MindUp, currently provide mindfulness activities and lesson plans for teachers. Could we create a different "mindfulness" program, product, or service?

WHO else could benefit from mindfulness training? Students in business schools? Medical schools? Nurses? Patients in pain? New, stressed-out parents? ADD Kids? Sports coaches and their teams? Firefighters? Police officers? The military? Divinity schools? Airline pilots? Customer service personnel in corporations? HR executives? College freshman as part of their orientation? Anyone dealing with the public?

WHAT aspect of mindfulness is being taught? Scientifically validated approaches? Exercises that specifically lower blood pressure? Settle stomachs? To help one sleep? Lose weight (less eating to combat stress)? Reduce drugs or alcohol? Exercises to develop specific skills: Writing? Public speaking? Creativity?

WHEN could mindfulness being taught? Could there be specific exercises for different times of the day? Waking up? Mid-afternoon instead of drinking coffee? Late at night? When traveling? At transitional moments in life: graduating school, starting a new job, getting married for both the bride and groom, starting a new job, retiring, having a baby, at the death of a loved one?

WHERE could mindfulness programs be introduced besides schools? At the gym? Health clubs? Kid's summer camps? Drug and alcohol rehab facilities? Prisons? Congress? Highly stressful business environments? At coaching clinics? In the car? At the airport?

WHY mindfulness? To reduce crime, drug use, obesity, suicides, bullying? Help disadvantaged people? Increase the nation's health? Train workers more effectively, faster, and cheaper? Lessen job accidents/fatalities? Improve safety? Promote world peace? Help retirees be happier/more productive? Increase family harmony? Lower the divorce rate?

HOW can a new "mindfulness" business or nonprofit organization be created? How could it be funded? Scientifically validated? Popularized? Could a celebrity become a spokesperson for a new mindfulness program, much like celebrities now endorse beauty products, weight loss, and exercise programs?

It's not hard to imagine dozens of new services and products that could be created by the answers—and the combining of the answers—to these questions.

Could you use the same "5 W's and H" technique against new product trends as well? Absolutely! Here are four food and beverage trends, again from the JWT reports:

1. Infused Ice Cubes: "cubes of different shapes and sizes that are made with juices, fruits, syrups, and herbs."
2. Bone Broth: The Hot New beverage… "it's nourishing, simple, cheap, and tastes amazing."
3. Charcoal: Juices containing charcoal "help trap chemicals and stop them from being absorbed into the skin."
4. "Franken-food" as I call it: Faux meat, eggless mayo, "beef crumble" made with pea protein, vegan cookies, "tomatoes that mimic tuna," etc.

Your assignment for today is to take one of the social or product trends above (or maybe one of your own) and create several unique new products and/or services by "bending these trends" with the "5 W's and H" technique.

DAY #16:
SAVING THE WORST FOR LAST

Let's say the Trend Bending exercise has inspired you to create and market an innovative new line of food or beverage products, but bone broth, vegan cookies, or spiced ice cubes just aren't doing it for you.

Maybe you follow the lead of Jim Goldberg, CEO and founder of Deep River Snacks, who, with his training as a lawyer and a chef, focused on unique flavors and created a line of kettle-cooked potato chips.

Or maybe, like Brownie Brittle founder and CEO "Sheila G" Mains who snacked on the crispy chocolate drippings on the side of her brownie cooking pans and decided to "bring the best part of the brownie to market," you find a new lighter and healthier form for an old favorite.

Or possibly, like former investment banker, Mario Leite, you mash together two things you love—tea and ice cream—and create the light and delicious "Tea-rrific" new line of ice cream and sorbets with tea as its main ingredient.

So what's your pleasure? Creating a new kind of French fry? A new, more flavorful meat marinade? A more exotic line of jellies or preserves? Bean-based "potato" chips?

A concept that receives record scores when we test it in focus groups are food or drinks that help moms get a full serving of vegetables into their kids. And it almost doesn't matter the category: bread, yogurt, desserts of all kinds—if the taste (and occasionally the color, too) of the vegetables can be disguised enough so the kids will eat or drink it, it's a winner. Juices, in particular, have jumped on this vegetable-serving-a-day bandwagon, right?

Could soups do the same? Certainly they could, maybe with an even tastier product? The start-up Soupure sells soups that are high in fiber and vitamins to help people lose weight. Exotic flavor combinations include zucchini basil and strawberry cashew. Brooklyn-based The Splendid Spoon sells soups with two or more servings of vegetables with such exotic varieties as butternut turmeric and sweet and spicy beet.

And the healthy meal delivery service Real Food Works of Los Angeles offers a one-day soup detox program of six different soups including kale, cauliflower, cucumber, melon, and mint that have the advantages of a detox program but without the high fructose in most juice cleanses.

How might you generate a unique idea in the world of soups? Probably one of the more surprising—and successful—techniques we use in our client ideation sessions is one we call the "Worst Idea technique." As its name implies, you begin this technique by generating a list of not good ideas, but instead the worst idea you can possibly think of in your category of interest.

These "worst ideas" should be truly awful, stupid, ridiculous, politically incorrect, sexually inappropriate, weird, disgusting and/or gross. (If this is a corporate ideation session, tell HR they can't come!)

After you create worst ideas—often twenty or more so that you move beyond relatively tame worst ideas you might create at the start of the exercise to the truly awful ones that can show up at the end of the exercise—you then turn these ideas into good or even great ideas. How do you do this? The obvious strategy is to do the exact opposite. The challenge is that the opposite may be neither obvious nor particularly productive. If your worst idea is a line "extra-watery" soups, then thinking of the opposite, "low-water soups," isn't particularly helpful or inspiring.

Typically, the more interesting strategy is to ask, as bad as the idea is, is there anything I can take out of it and turn it into a good idea? Now, extra-watery soup is a pretty tame worst idea (as we'll see shortly) but even so it might inspire some new thinking about the category. Could you, for instance, design a line of on-the-go, cold soups with extra-high water content—and even added electrolytes— that would make it a refreshing, light and nourishing meal replacement? Smoothies beware, here come "Souper Soups."

If "extra-watery" soup isn't bad enough, what could be some truly terrible ideas? Here are twenty:

1. "Snot" soup
2. Soup that makes you exhausted or worse yet, catatonic
3. Soup that makes you throw up

4. Soup made with radioactive waste
5. Soup with baby placentas in it
6. Soup that donates a portion of its sales to terrorists
7. Soup that can double as a floor wax (Or a dessert topping? See the Saturday Night Live archives.)
8. Aphrodisiac/orgasm soup
9. Soup with absolutely no taste
10. "Celebrity soup" from the Grand Wizard of the Ku Klux Klan
11. Soup sold only after its expiration date (with a botulism side car)
12. Soup that helps dieters *gain* weight
13. Laxative soup
14. Soup that will give you the flu
15. Soup that erases your short-term memory
16. Soup for dogs
17. Soup that makes you spastic
18. Soup with dirt—and rocks—in it
19. Soup that comes in a dishwashing detergent bottle

And, of course…

20. Soup created by (and for?) Nazi's. (See Seinfeld episode)

Pretty bad. For this technique to be its most effective, it's very important to push yourself to be truly terrible. Then the fun of trying to turn worst to best can begin. Let's try it with the first two ideas.

"Snot soup" might inspire a line of kid's soups (yes, with a full supply of vegetables), that is intentionally "gross" or "horrific," especially for younger boys. It might include body parts floating in (tomato) blood. Or, maybe the bigger idea is a line of soups inspired and endorsed by TV shows, networks, or movies. Certainly, a Nickelodeon, green (pea) slime soup could be a winner!

"Soup that makes you exhausted or catatonic," could be a special line of easy-to-digest nighttime soups that, like warm milk, help you fall asleep naturally without the need for sleeping pills.

You get the idea.

If you know the area in which you would like to invent a new product or service, the Worst Idea technique should help you discover and invent ideas you might never have thought of otherwise. I've certainly found this to be true in our client ideation sessions, whether it was creating a new line of food products, or an international banking service, or a patented line of tools, or a new data and information services division.

Your assignment for today: focus on one of your areas of entrepreneurial interest and passion and use the Worst Idea technique to generate at least three (anything but worst), great new ideas!

DAY #17:
FINAL EXAM: BRINGING IT ALL TOGETHER

In addition to consulting on innovation projects to help our clients create, develop, and launch "the next big thing," clients also ask us to train their high-potential, or early-in-career executives, how to think more imaginatively and be better creative problem solvers.

The final technique we teach in our two-day program is Mindmapping. If you're not familiar with Mindmapping, it's an especially valuable creative thinking tool for creating presentations, visualizing complicated projects, and capturing thoughts in such a way that they will be more likely to: a) be remembered later and b) be combined with other ideas/thoughts to create new ideas in the future. Think of a Mindmap as a kind of multi-colored tree diagram, with key words (not sentences) and pictures on the tree's branches. (See Mindmapping.com for more information about both how and when to use Mindmapping.)

Why do we leave Mindmapping for the very end of the creativity workshop? Because, it allows us to essentially kill two birds with one stone. We demonstrate the how-to's of Mindmapping by creating a Mindmap of everything we've covered in the workshop for the past two days. So, not only do the session participants learn how to do Mindmapping, they also get a memorable review and map of the workshop's two-day content.

In the same spirit of being creative about reviewing creative processes—in a sense turning the process on itself—let's apply the nine creative techniques we've learned in the past eight days to the inventive challenge of teaching inventing. Specifically, let's create a variety of "minds-on" exhibits for a new museum I'm calling The Inventors' Workshop.

What were the creative techniques we covered in the past eight days? Wishing, Questioning Assumptions, Twenty Questions, the "And" technique (which was similar to Benefit Word Mashing), Idea Hooks, Trend Bending, Patent Prompts, and Worst Idea technique.

What are some *trends* in modern-day museum exhibits but also in other entertainment venues—Broadway shows, sporting events, parades, amusement parks—that might help us think of some ideas or evolve preliminary ideas into even better ones?

Interactivity is a trend for sure. Robots, animatronics, and more life-like characters and realistic environments—real or virtual—are, too. Play and "gamification" are hot. So are 3D effects and 3D printers. How could smart technology provide a better learning and more memorable museum experience? What about personalization or customization?

Storytelling? Can we create a story or journey to unite different elements of The Inventors' Workshop exhibit into an overall theme?

What are some *assumptions* we make about museum exhibits? We assume...

1) You walk through them. 2) They are for people. 3) The people visiting the exhibit are not part of the exhibit. 4) They are educational in some way. 5) There is a natural flow/progression in the exhibit: a beginning, middle, and end. 6) People can see and hear and feel things when they go through the exhibit. 7) Visitors can read. 8) They are limited by gravity. 9) They are not designed to be frustrating. 10) They cost money.

What are some of the *twenty questions* we might ask about The Inventors' Workshop?

1) How could we get people inside the mind of an inventor? 2) How could we have people experience a eureka moment by discovering or inventing something new? 3) How could we show what it's really like to be an inventor, including both the successes and the failures? 4) How can we show people inventing is sometimes as much about identifying problems as it is about solving them? 5) How could we include real world inventive challenges in the exhibit? 6) How can we demonstrate the use of visual or design thinking in inventing? 7) How could we make the exhibit fun by making it a game in some way? 8) How could we make invention more approachable, so everyone feels like they can

do it? 9) How can we design interactive inventive experiences for young and old alike? 10) How can we show inventions in every aspect of life?

"And," what are some words we might link to the word invention that might inspire some new exhibit ideas? How about if we combine "invention" with different disciplines and/or arenas of interest?

Invention and...literature, economics, philosophy, biology, medicine, history, sports, games, art, writing, storytelling, cartoons, movies, drawing, words, TV shows, heroes, women, souvenirs, photography, newspapers, demographics/age groups, corporations, technology, patents, different cultures, timelines, and connections.

What might we "*idea hook*" onto to create a great Inventors' Workshop? The 9/11 memorial? A performance by the Blue Man group? The Smithsonian Museums? A Disney World Exhibit? The Tower of Terror? The Macy's Thanksgiving Day Parade? Joseph Campbell's *The Hero's Journey*?

What *patents* can *prompt* ideas on presenting patents? Besides including reproductions of actual patents in the "Inventors' Workshop," how might patent abstracts themselves trigger several new exhibit ideas? What if we keyword searched the United States Patent and Trademark Office for: "Games" or "Toys?" "Fun" or "Entertainment?"

What *benefits* might we *mashup* to inspire several new ideas? How could we use smart technology in a museum exhibit? Speed/quickness? Leverage educational best practices? Impart information in new and different ways? Use virtual reality?

How about using *worst ideas* to inspire ideas for The Inventors' Workshop museum? A museum that: 1) has nothing in it, 2) kicks out people who talk, 3) has an admission fee of $100,000, 4) teaches people how to be braindead/not have original ideas, 5) has historical profiles of inventors that are intentionally inaccurate, 6) makes great inventors seem like idiots, 7) is only open for 60 seconds a day, 8) only allows college students admission, 9) only displays inventions that were used for torture throughout history, and 10) only features inventions that failed/never made it to market.

What about some *wishes?* I wish this new Inventors' Workshop Museum...

> 1) could help people of all ages who go to it to invent something new, 2) would make inventing so cool that great inventors became true heroes to kids, 3) could raise millions for teaching inventing in the US and around the world, 4) had both a physical and a virtual presence, 5) was worthy of a cover story in *Time*, a documentary, and featured on 60 Minutes, 6) invented and popularized state-of-the-art creative thinking techniques, 7) had a number of games and toys on the market that were inspired by it, 8) was affiliated with a university, or corporation sponsoring research on inventive thinking, 9) was a model for other invention museums around the world, 10) helped aspiring inventors develop prototypes for their inventions.

So, now with all this creative technique and stimuli groundwork done, it makes it easy to start generating some

"Inventors' Workshop" museum exhibit ideas.

The worst idea of making "inventors seem like idiots" might inspire an idea for a fun section in the museum of "crazy ideas" from inventors. Henry Ford used to dye his hair with rusty water. George Eastman, inventor of the Kodak camera, supported the thirteen month calendar. Edison thought there were sub-microscopic entities, or "little people" living in his brain. Nikola Tesla, inventor of the AC electric motor (and presumably a hero of Tesla car inventor Elon Musk), once tried to invent a device to photograph thoughts on the retina of the eye.

Linking "invention" and "TV shows" in the "And" technique might inspire an exhibit reminiscent of the old TV series MacGyver, in which the secret-agent star of the show drew on a "vast practical knowledge of science," that enabled him to "make use of any mundane materials around him to create unorthodox solutions to any problem" he faced. Not unlike the scene in the movie Apollo 13 where NASA engineers jury-rig a device to filter out $CO2$ from the disabled spacecraft, our museum could include a wide variety of tools and "mundane materials" (duct tape surely among them) to create solutions to a wide variety of pre-arranged challenges/problems.

The wish for "corporate or university sponsors" might spark the idea of different companies subsidizing exhibits detailing the history of invention both in their company and their industry.

The question, "How could we include real world inventive challenges in the exhibit?" might mean that these same sponsoring companies could use "crowdsourcing" at the museum and ask for suggestions about how to improve products they are about to launch.

The assumption that the people visiting the exhibit are not part of the exhibit might suggest that the modern-day inventors could be guests of the museum, either in person or virtually, to talk about how they created their inventions and answer questions from museum attendees.

The trend toward personalization? Storytelling? Idea hooking off the "hero's journey"? Maybe exhibit-goers rotate through a series of inventors' stations, with different creativity exercises (similar to the ones in this book?) at each station that help them create new inventions in their particular area of interest? Maybe there are even 3D printers at the end of this heroic "inventors' journey" that could create a prototype or model of their invention? If some great inventions were created, maybe the "worst idea" of charging a $100,000 admission fee isn't that crazy, after all.

The assignment for today: spend several hours working through all nine creativity techniques to create at least three new big ideas in your areas of passion.

SECTION #4:
CHOOSING, DEVELOPING, AND CREATIVELY SELLING YOUR BIGGEST IDEAS

DAY #18:
A SIMPLE CONCEPT DEVELOPMENT
TECHNIQUE: BILLBOARDING

So you and your innovation team have a variety of big ideas you're excited about pursuing further. What's next?

Over the years I have experimented with different ways to help our clients develop preliminary ideas into better-thought-out concepts. After much trial and error, a technique we invented called Billboarding[1] has proven itself to be a simple, effective, and fun way to:

1. help the ideation team preliminarily determine an idea's potential by

2. identifying its most important benefit for consumers or customers.

---

1 If you're interested in how we invented the Billboard Technique, an article I wrote for FastCompany.com tells the story. Read "To Promote a New Idea, Forget the Powerpoint, Try a Billboard," by visiting: www.fastcompany.com/3003484/promote-new-idea-forget-powerpoint-try-billboard.

Ideas that may have initially seemed quite exciting in the ideation session can turn out to be less so after Billboarding when the team discovers the idea's anticipated consumer benefit simply is not new, unique, or compelling.

Conversely, teams that have Billboarded good, but not necessarily great, ideas from the ideation session have, on occasion, realized that they do indeed have a breakthrough concept, because the consumer (or customer) benefit is so original and important.

Think of Billboarding as a kind of "elevator speech" for your new idea. Like a typical highway sign, the billboard you'll create for each of your big ideas will include three elements: a headline, a visual, and a tag line or reason to believe. Here's how you do it.

Step one. Figure out exactly what the idea is. Often preliminary ideas need to be developed a bit further before they can be billboarded. Think about how the idea could actually work, as well as giving the idea/product/service a name.

Step two. List all the benefits of the idea. In most cases, you should be able to think of at least five or six benefits of your idea. If this is an invention, product, or service for consumers, then make sure you're listing the benefits to an imagined consumer. If this is a business-to-business product or service, then the benefits are for the customer (either the specific buyer at the organization or the organization itself).

Step three. Pick what you think is the single most important benefit from your list of benefits, and create a short headline that communicates this benefit. By the way, you're not trying to be particularly clever with your headline (i.e., making it rhyme). You're trying to be clear!

Step four. Create a visual that communicates the key benefit (or one of the important features) of the idea.

Step five. Create a tagline with a reason to believe in it.

So, to use an everyday example: Here are some of the benefits, listed on the Amazon website, of the Bounty paper towel.

- Stronger when wet, so you can rinse it, reuse it, and throw it away
- Absorbs faster than any other paper towel so you can get the job done right the first time
- Lets you thoroughly clean and then throw the towel away, removing the potential breeding ground for germs
- Classic white color to complement any décor

Students of advertising or the afternoon soap operas will remember that P & G launched the paper towel highlighting the second benefit:

- *Headline*: Bounty, The Quicker Picker Upper. (Okay, so this headline actually did rhyme.)
- The accompanying *visual*: Paper towel absorbing a spill.
- And the modern-day *Reason to Believe*: "Bounty features unique Trap & Lock Technology that quickly picks up liquid messes."

Let's do one more example, this time from my own 21-day experiment. You'll remember the inexpensive cardboard bicycle from Day 3. Of all twenty plus preliminary ideas I considered for this technology, the one I chose to think about further was the stroller. Exclusive of the idea I came up with to make the cardboard stroller concept unique, here are some of the obvious features and benefits:

For a consumer:

- Because it's lighter, it makes it easier to transport and carry.
- It's lightweight which makes it less likely to injure yourself or the child if you drop it.
- Being inexpensive could make it more convenient: you can keep one in the car and one at home.
- Inexpensive means better fit for the child: you can afford to get new, larger strollers as the child grows.
- The safer stroller: because cardboard "gives," (unlike rigid plastic or metal), it protects your child from injury/whiplash if you bang into something.

For a customer:

- Inexpensive enough to provide them a fleet of free or rentable strollers for shoppers at your mall or theme park
- Can easily be customized with advertisements and/or stickers

Does this final customer benefit trigger in you any other ideas for a new kind of stroller? What about the idea that cardboard can easily be drawn on?

That thought led me to the idea of a "Playhouse Stroller" and a unique benefit for both mom (or dad) and the child. Here's the billboard:

- Headline: The Playhouse Stroller: When You're

Shopping, They're Having Fun, Too!
- Visual: Smiling child in the cardboard Playhouse Stroller having fun drawing and placing stickers on the stroller.
- Reason-to-Believe: Comes with a 120 Crayola crayons and over 1000 stickers so your child can use his or her creative imagination... anytime, anywhere!

The Billboard Technique helps you be explicit about the benefits to consumers and/or customers of your new idea. And in the process, you should become that much more excited about the idea's potential.

How will you know if you're pursuing the best big idea? That's what we'll look at next. But first, your assignment for today is to go through each step of the Billboarding process and create a billboard for one of your favorite ideas.

DAY #19:
RESEARCHING AND DEVELOPING
YOUR FAVORITE IDEAS

At my innovation agency, we evangelize to our clients constantly and practice daily our passionately held belief that successful innovation begins and ends with the consumer/customer. Consumers vote with their pocketbooks every day. Customers stake their reputations, and occasionally their careers, on knowing and deciding which products and services will best serve their organization's goals.

How do you create products and services to best meet the needs of both consumers and customers? The simple answer is: by speaking with people.

As innovation consultants to large companies, "speaking with people," in our case, includes moderating conventional focus groups, as well as conducting in-depth, one-on-one interviews, shop alongs, home-use tests, in- and out-of-home ethnographies, and online surveys.

In recent years, it's become fashionable to dismiss the importance and effectiveness of consumer research in general and focus groups in particular. I suspect this is because many focus groups are used incorrectly. They should not be seen as a substitute for decision making and leadership, but rather as an invitation to learning. As one of our clients so eloquently put it, "focus groups help me sharpen my gut." At the end of the day, it's the experienced gut that should decide on the way forward, not a few consumers on the other side of a two-way mirror in Columbus, Ohio.

Focus groups can help intrapreneurs and entrepreneurs gain critical insights into the most important points of difference of their idea, and how to price, package, position, and promote it. But what if you or your team have neither the experience nor the money to conduct a day of focus groups (i.e., three two-hour groups with eight consumers per group), which with the moderator fees, facility costs, recruitment fees, participant incentives, client meals, video-recording, and transcription can cost $20,000 or more per day?

The answer is that, with a few best practices, you don't necessarily have to go through the expense of doing formal focus groups. By being creative and resourceful, you can achieve many of the same insights and learnings with little or no cost. How? Turns out people, even relative strangers, are more than willing to tell you what they think of your idea.

I remember one time when we were trying to determine the best "kid" flavors for a line of prepackaged mini-bagels from Thomas. We didn't have the budget to do formal research, so I went to the principal of my son's public elementary school and asked if we could have 4th, 5th, and 6th graders taste test the different varieties we were considering. The principal agreed. We had to get permission from the parents, of course, but this was relatively easy. Teachers sent a permission slip home with a listing of all the ingredient and nutrition information on the products we wanted the kids to sample. Over fifty of the elementary schools kids participated in our informal test and filled out short surveys. The Thomas' blueberry mini-bagel was a big winner, and is still on the market today.

With a little creativity, qualitative research doesn't have to be expensive. We could also have tested the mini-bagels at say, a summer camp, or the YMCA.

In addition to the obvious choice of friends and family, other possibilities for testing different kinds of products and services could include: associations, nonprofits/charities, colleges or universities, executive education programs, the local firehouse, garden clubs, executive networking groups, your church (at a potluck dinner if you're testing a new food or beverage), and LinkedIn contacts, to name just a few.

What are some of best practices in testing new ideas? Three examples from our innovation consulting work help illustrate several important things to think about when you use consumers and customers to test your ideas.

BEST PRACTICE #1: CREATE PROTOTYPES, EVEN RUDIMENTARY ONES

Consumers seldom can tell you what they want. Henry Ford's quote, "If I had asked people what they wanted, they would have said faster horses," comes to mind. But they can tell you what they like and don't like if you present them with something specific to react to. And the more concrete you can make your idea, the more likely you will get the feedback and learning you are looking for. Just as the creative mind needs diverse stimuli to create a continuous stream of new and original ideas, the analytical mind also needs concrete things to react to. So, when you're looking to test your idea, create prototypes, even very inexpensive ones, to help you get the learning you need.

Case in point is a project we did for Dr. Scholl's. The idea was to create an insole that would have special vents to keep feet cool and dry in the summer. Consumers were interested, but it wasn't until we created prototypes they could react to that we got the in-depth insights that we were looking for. Dr. Scholl's Dreamwalk Fresh and Cool Insoles have cutouts to promote airflow, as well as a moisture-wicking, breathable top cloth. When consumers saw our handmade prototypes—even though they were very basic and made out of cardboard, cloth, and paper—it was easy for them to tell us what they wanted, and didn't want, in the product's design. Turns out having both the vents to keep feet cool and the moisture-wicking top cloth to keep feet dry were critical to the product's success.

BEST PRACTICE #2: TALK WITH DIFFERENT PEOPLE AT DIFFERENT TIMES AS YOU DEVELOP YOUR IDEA

On all of our innovation consulting projects, we bring research and idea-generation expertise, new ideas, and the experience from having led over two hundred successful innovation projects creating, developing, and marketing new ideas. But we also assume that the client will always know more about their business than we ever will. We have to make sure we are always leveraging and evolving our clients' significant knowledge.

We were asked by the makers of Craftsman tools and Sears to help them: a) determine why sales of their ratchets, wrenches and sockets sets were not growing, b) reimagine how these sets could be more effectively merchandised and displayed in their stores, and c) invent new products/sets to help grow the business.

So, the question became: how could we educate both ourselves and our client quickly about the unmet consumer needs—and therefore opportunities—there might be in the ratchets, wrenches, and sockets product categories? We needed to talk with consumers, but not just any consumers. It's the most experienced users who can provide greatest insight in the shortest amount of time—into both the category itself and your products within that category. In the case of the ratchets, wrenches, and sockets, this meant either professional mechanics or very experienced do-it-yourselfers. Think of the neighbor who's always working on his car in the driveway on the weekends.

I've always said that it's amazing what you can learn by talking with people, and this is especially true of experienced users.

Once you've gotten yourself grounded in the category, then it's time to branch out and speak to different potential target markets. For current and potential ratchet, wrench, and socket users, this meant we spoke to younger and older men, women, new homeowners, Hispanic men (whom we were told will sometimes create a social and/or family event of repairing a car), and "tuners," or guys who were tricking out their cars. We learned, among other things, that with the popularity of do-it-yourself books, blogs, and TV shows, women now wanted their own sets of tools. And men wanted multiple sets: for their car, in the workshop, even specially-customized sets for their motorcycle or boat, etc. All this learning led not only to the successful introduction of a wide variety of new ratchets, wrenches, and socket sets, a 6% increase in sales, and an unprecedented six vendor awards, but a complete redesign of the section in all Sears stores to make it easier to find and select the set that was "right for you."

BEST PRACTICE #3: WATCH PEOPLE USE YOUR PRODUCT

An important trend in consumer research is to get out of the artificial environment of a focus group facility and go to where people are actually using the product. For us, this means we will often go to people's homes to do one-on-one interviews. For the successful development of the Gray Solutions hair-coloring product, for instance, we conducted in-home interviews with women and asked them to pretend/role play every step in their home hair-coloring routine.

These at-home "ethnographies," as they are known, are particularly valuable when you are trying to design easy-to-use products and packages, write clear directions for how to use a product, and identify why consumers think the product could be superior to others currently on the market.

A good example of the importance (and power) of seeing consumers use the product in a real-life environment was research we did for a new product from Prestone: a 2-in-1 car wash and wax. The product was an emulsion of silicone and carnauba wax so that you could "wax every time you wash."

We knew that it was important for the entire innovation team to see and talk with consumers as they used the product if we were going to understand how to communicate its point of difference. So we set up mini-car washes in the parking lot of a focus group facility and recruited guys with dirty cars to come in and wash and wax their cars while we interviewed and videotaped them about every aspect of their car washing and waxing experience.

The key to making these interviews productive was to be extremely detailed about every facet of the product and the process for using it: before, during, and after washing and waxing. What was the first thing they noticed about the package? Did it fit in the hand correctly? Did it open easily? Were the instructions for use clear? What about the package visual? How about the name? Did the package copy communicate the product's key points of difference? Was it clear that the product should be applied to a wet car?

As they used the product, did it go on easily? How did it compare to the way they'd typically wash and wax their car? Any surprises? Disappointments? Special advantages?

After they were done, what did they think of the result? Were they happy with the shine? Did the water bead the way they expected it would? Did it save them time? Would they buy it? Pay a premium? How often would they use it?

Now that they'd used the product, what was the most

important thing to communicate about it? Would they change the name? Modify the directions for use? Suggest a different visual for the front of the package?

By keeping an open, almost childlike, curiosity in every phase of the interview, consumers were invited to become true design and communication partners in the development of this successful new product.

The name: Prestone Water Activated Carnauba Liquid Wax.

Some of the great messaging that consumers helped us create:

- "Wax every time you wash."
- "Silicone enables the water spray to 'do the waxing for you.'"
- "Fills in micro-scratches."
- "Water does the buffing for you."
- "Goes on clean. Comes off clean. Minimal elbow grease required."
- "Shine and protection for up to six weeks."

I'll say it again. It's amazing what you can learn by talking with people.

Your assignment for today is to start talking with some potential users for your new product or service. As you do this, please remember that your job now is to learn, not defend. This is a unique opportunity to find out what you can improve in your new product or service, not explain to people why you are right. This is the time for asking questions and listening objectively to what you're hearing.

DAY #20:
BUSINESS BUILDING TECHNIQUES:
LET'S GET VISUAL

So, let's say you've created a Billboard to help clarify what makes your idea different for a specific target market. That's step one. If it's a new service you're creating, besides knowing who might be most likely to buy it and why, you'll also need to know how your new service will be popularized, promoted, distributed, priced, and sold. If it's a new product, beyond everything you'd do for a service, you'll also need to decide on how and where the product (and its ingredients) will be designed, engineered, manufactured and packaged. And regardless of whether it's a product or service you'll also, of course, need a name.

Besides the billboard, there are a variety of visually oriented creative techniques that can help you further develop your preliminary idea into a well-thought-out business proposition. These techniques can all be used as part of what we call a "creative war room."

THE CREATIVE WAR ROOM

Not long ago, we were asked to lead a worldwide innovation project for a well-known pain reliever. The assignment was particularly challenging because we'd be creating ideas for eighteen different countries/regions around the world, all with very different cultures, and therefore presumably different solutions. To complicate things further, we were tasked with not only generating ideas for new product line extensions, but new packaging, merchandising, promotion, PR, and distribution concepts as well. Money and time were short. We didn't have the luxury of traveling to each country to individually work with each local office/team to generate these new ideas.

Our solution was to design and facilitate a global virtual ideation process that used the local offices to both generate the idea-provoking stimuli for the entire worldwide team… as well as create the winning, specific ideas for each country.

We began the project by having the company's local marketers and researchers take pictures of everything from where and how their product was currently displayed and distributed, how it was stored in the home and used by consumers, and places (other than a pharmacy) where it might be sold. We also asked that everyone "think outside of the category" and take pictures or send us written summaries of any other interesting promotions, ads, products, packages, or merchandising concepts—not from the world of pain relief that they thought might help creatively inspire the global team.

You can imagine that with dozens of marketers and researchers from around the world contributing, the stimuli quickly became overwhelming. So, we built a creative war room where we arranged the contributed pictures and ideas on the walls of our company's conference room, and used it as the basis for our own preliminary idea generation and planning. We also emailed photos of provocative "wall collages" we had created from the submitted stimuli to trigger a wide variety of ideas from each of the worldwide offices. And finally, we used the contributed stimuli as special "thought starters" for a variety of ideation techniques we led the global team through—again, all delivered and facilitated virtually—over an intense four-week period of new idea generation.

The results were extraordinary both for the breadth and depth of the new product, marketing, promotion, merchandising, and distribution ideas generated for each local market. (Consider that in India pain relievers are often only sold in one or two tablet packs because the poorer families cannot afford to buy the one-hundred count bottles we take for granted in the US, and you can begin to imagine how different the winning ideas were for each country.)

There are many advantages to using a whiteboard, corkboard, entire wall, or if you have the space, as Google Ventures does for it design projects, an entire room dedicated to your new venture. (Google Ventures, as I recently learned, also calls these dedicated creativity centers "creative war rooms." See GV.com/library for more information.) Being able to visualize all the components of your big idea in a single place can be extremely helpful. You can see both the big idea "big picture," as well as the details of your new business or product concept at the same time.

How might you use a "creative war room" for the development of your big idea? It can be both a creative planning and project prioritization tool, and a team idea-generation vehicle and recording medium. And don't worry about how the project components are "organized": often the more random the better, since the randominity makes it more likely you'll discover exciting and new connections between seemingly unrelated elements.

As a work in progress, you'll want to fill your idea wall or board with everything from prototype drawings to magazines images that capture the look and feel of your product or service; names you are considering to pictures of people who represent your ideal target market(s); key insights and strategic directions already decided on, to finance questions yet to be answered; potentially exciting marketing, merchandising, and sales concepts to PR and social media directions in need of additional thinking and inspiration. The simple act of externalizing all these elements and moving them out of your head and onto a wall will help you and your team crystalize your idea and know its critical success factors. By committing your big idea to this physical and visual form, it will begin to become that much more real.

Visualizing all these components of your big idea will also enable you to leverage "soak time." This is giving your pattern-finding, subconscious mind the time it needs to make surprising intuitive connections, identify patterns, and make important creative leaps among the different elements on your idea wall.

Having trouble finding a name for your product or service you love? In addition to creating new names by combing words from names you've already considered, you might be surprised that it could be a posted visual—say of a particular target market customer—and not a combination of words that could inspire the winning name.

Haven't yet found the sleek design for your new product? Do what one of the car companies did when designing a new car: they created a creative design war room and posted cool designs from everything but cars as inspiration: from skis to pens, wristwatches to sneakers.

Having trouble seeing the forest for the trees? Do what Imagineers did when designing Disneyland. They adapted the storyboard technique that they had used to visualize each scene of their animated features to storyboard/visualize the entire park, and, in the process, allowed Walt to quickly see the progress at each stage of the Park's design and construction.

So create your own creative war room for whatever creative development challenges you and your team are now facing.

DAY #21:
GENERATING SELLING CONCEPTS:
THE OPPORTUNITY REDEFINITION TECHNIQUE

In my last book, I told the story of how a company I consulted with, a Midwest insurance company, used the opportunity redefinition technique to increase their sales by 52% in less than a year.

I want to share the opportunity redefinition technique with you now because, of all the techniques in this book, it's probably the most helpful for generating creative ways to promote and market your new big idea. Indeed, how you're planning to market your product or service might be as critical to the ultimate success of your concept product or service as the original idea itself. Your go-to market strategy might **be** the idea.

When we teach this technique in our creativity and ideation training sessions, nobody can quite believe:

- How universally applicable the technique is, not only for generating new selling ideas, but for solving other creative challenges as well
- How truly easy it is to learn: fewer than ten minutes at most
- That in their entire educational experience, from elementary school to business school, they were never taught such a simple and powerful technique

The problem redefinition technique, as its name implies, helps you to redefine your problem or challenge from one that initially might have seemed limited or constrained to one with literally unlimited possibilities. You do this by creating word alternatives in your original problem redefinition.

To demonstrate, let's take the I-MONE (International Medical Options Network) idea I shared on Day 7. You'll remember, this was an international vetting and referral service for US residents to have operations performed in foreign countries at a much reduced cost.

So, your entrepreneurial problem/challenge might be defined as simply as: "How do I promote I-MONE to prospective patients?"

To do the opportunity redefinition technique, takes three simple steps.

1. Pick three words in the sentence—typically the subject, verb, and object—and generate alternatives for each selected word.
2. Rewrite the sentence by randomly combining the alternative words.

3. Use the redefined sentence to trigger new ideas or ways of looking at the challenge.

So the three selected words in our sentence could be: "How do *I promote* I-MONE to prospective *patients?*"

What then, are some alternatives for the word "I"? How about:

> 1) Investors, 2) Family, 3) Friends, 4) Nurses, 5) Doctors, 6) Hospitals, 7) Insurance Companies, 8) Clinics, 9) Taxpayers, 10) Medicare, 11) Foreign Hospitals, 12) Travel Agencies

Other options for the word "promote"?

> 1) Sell, 2) Co-market, 3) Give away, 4) License, 5) Incentivize, 6) Advertise, 7) Publicize, 8) Social "media-ize," 9) Network, 10) Telemarket, 11) Reward, 12) Test

And finally, alternative, possibly even more specific, ways to think of "patients"?

> 1) Retirees, 2) Athletes, 3) Parents, 4) College Kids, 5) Accident Victims, 6) Children, 7) Organ Donors, 8) Tourists, 9) Expatriates, 11) Celebrities, 11) Siblings, 12) Weekend Warriors

So, when we start randomly combining words from each of the three lists, we might get such thought-provoking questions such as:

- How do *doctors incentivize* using I-MONE to *parents?*
- How do *doctors network* I-MONE to *tourists?*
- How do *insurance companies co-market* I-MONE

to *accident victims?*

- How do *foreign hospitals reward* using I-MONE to *celebrities?*
- How do *travel agencies publicize* I-MONE to *retirees?*

How many redefined sentences can we generate from these varied word options? If you said a lot, you're right: Seventeen-hundred twenty-eight (12 x 12 x 12) to be exact. Of course, if we had had twenty options for each of the three words, there would have been a lot more: 8,000 possible ways to redefine the sentence.

The final step is to use these redefined sentences as thought prompts to create innovative ways to sell, market, and/or promote your new service. The fifth redefined sentence: "How do *travel agencies publicize* I-MONE to *retirees?*" implies a particularly interesting market and promotion strategy, especially since retirees would be a prime target market for later-in-life operations. Why not do a joint marketing effort with either a US tourism company (i.e., Perillo, AARP, Viking European River cruises), an airline, or a country's tourism bureau promoting lower-cost, overseas medical procedures? The money saved by having one's operation in a foreign country could not only pay for the operation and the airfare to get there, but a two or three-week vacation as well. One can imagine an ad for this new service: "Take a *Free* Walking Tour of Europe's Great Cities—on Your New Knee!" It could be a wonderful way for a concerned wife to convince her stoic husband to finally get that knee replacement surgery he's been putting off for the past two years.

There are three things to keep in mind when you do

the opportunity redefinition technique. First, and most important, is to recognize that these redefined questions are intended simply to "get you thinking." Seldom is there "an answer" that appears from these random combinations. As we tell our creativity training clients, you have to work these questions until you get an idea you like. And, in the process, you should feel free to go beyond what the question might imply. Two of the word alternatives could inspire you to create your new sales, promotion advertising, PR, or marketing idea. The idea police will never show up to arrest you for not using all or even most of the trigger words as inspiration. At the end of the day, it doesn't matter how you got your new marketing or promotion idea—just that you did!

Second, you have to appreciate that, like any ideation session, succeeding with the opportunity redefinition technique is a numbers game. Many of the redefined questions will not inspire a great new idea. But among the hundreds or thousands of possibilities there will certainly be several that do. Our insurance agency client, for example, had their marketing and sales teams work through literally hundreds of opportunity redefinitions to get to the half dozen ideas that were ultimately responsible for increasing their sales by 52%.

Finally, you may discover, as you work with the opportunity redefinition technique to generate new promotional or sales concepts for your big idea, that it might even inspire you to think of new business models, distribution concepts, or joint ventures that were not an essential feature of your initial big idea concept. The brilliance behind the Progressive Insurance "compare-prices-with-the-competition" ad campaign is not so much the trust it inspires with prospective consumers by offering to make this comparison—although this is certainly true. But rather, that it helps Progressive identify and presumably more aggressively market to lower-risk, potentially higher-profit-margin insurance customers. It's not hard to imagine how including a "low-risk/high-profit margin" target market as one of the options in the opportunity redefinition exercise could inspire this innovative marketing strategy and business model.

So might you try the opportunity redefinition technique? If my description of the technique, how easy it is to use, and how powerful the results can be still hasn't convinced you, allow me to share a story that will make it even easier than I've already explained.

As a Dartmouth Alumnus, the Alumni office will often contact me to see if I'd be willing to have an undergraduate intern at Growth Engine over the Christmas break. I almost always say yes. A couple of years ago, our intern, Hilton Hart, a junior, was a computer science major. I wasn't sure why he'd signed up to intern at a "marketing innovation agency," but I agreed nevertheless. Turns out we hit the jackpot.

In four weeks, we taught Hilton everything we could think of about ideation, creative qualitative research, and marketing innovation processes. In return, Hilton wrote a software program for us—consisting of over 1000 lines of code—for the opportunity redefinition technique. You'll find it on the Growth Engine website (www.growth-engine. com) under the "Idea Tools" tab, and it's free. Here's how it works: you type in the challenge you'd like to redefine, making sure that you have a question with a subject, verb, and object. Then you create/type in ten different options for each of these parts of speech. The program will then randomly combine your word options to create thought-provoking sentences. It will continue making these random combinations, ten at a time, until you reach the 1,000 possible permutations.

Your assignment for today: generate dozens of questions to help inspire new ideas for marketing and promoting your new business concept.

FINAL THOUGHTS

I've been asked in radio and print interviews the difference between ideation and innovation. My definitions are pretty simple. "Ideation" is coming up with new ideas. "Innovation" is the process of bringing those new ideas—hopefully successfully—to market.

It's important to know that the ideation and creative problem solving techniques I've explained and demonstrated in this book are equally as valid for generating ideas to solve the hundreds of challenges you'll encounter as you and your team work to innovate a new concept, as they are for creating your original "big idea." These creative innovation challenges could include generating out-of-the-box strategies for receiving corporate funding or raising venture capital, as well as creative ways to solve manufacturing, sales, marketing, and even logistics challenges.

The idea generation techniques in this book were included because they're easy to learn and apply and, most importantly, they work. Use them whenever and wherever you have a creative challenge, but especially when you come up against an "impossible challenge." The Wishing and Questioning Assumptions techniques should help you move beyond impossibilities to reframe and reimagine surprising but workable possibilities.

Other techniques can be used for different kinds of creative challenges. Twenty Questions and Patent Prompts can help you push your thinking on both the what and how of your favorite ideas. Trend Bending and Benefit Word Mashing will increase the odds that you're creating timely new ideas, even if you don't feel particularly tuned into the popular culture. The Worst Idea and "And" techniques are great reminders that big idea creation and innovation can and should be fun, even when you're dealing with the inevitable setbacks that come from creating something new to the world. Finally, Billboarding, Mindmapping, the creative war room, and the problem definition technique should help you successfully innovate your ideas.

The variety of idea creation and development techniques in this book means that you and your team should never feel stuck for the next big idea or creative breakthrough. Yes, big idea creation and innovation is hard work. But you now have the creative thinking tools you'll need to channel your passion and creativity into success. Good luck!